Published by Kate Macready

Copyright © Kate Macready 2017
ALL RIGHT RESERVED
FIRST PUBLISHED 2017

This book is copyright. Apart from any fair dealing for the purposes of private study, research, criticism or review, as permitted under the Copyright Act 1968, no part may be stored or reproduced by any process without prior written permission. Enquiries should be made to the publisher.

ISBN: 978-0-6482192-0-0

Cover image – photograph of their boat – *Elizabeth Jane II* at Kapingamarangi Atoll, Micronesia. Taken by the author.

Under the Arms of the Sky

A Sailing Adventure

By Kate Macready

Under the Arms of the Sky

We Come Here in Numbers 1

Leaving 9

In the Beginning 21

Getting into Our Sailing Groove 31

New Shores 43

The Spice Islands 55

Beneath the Surface 65

The Rainforest Island 75

Lightning 85

A Perfect Christmas 93

Encounter with a Rat 101

Friends and Goodbyes 109

Pirates! 117

Palau	129
'To Carry Under the Arms of the Sky'	143
Forever	161
The Church	169
Another Seven Hundred Miles	179
The Trade Economy	191
Coming Home	209
Post Script	223

About the Author

Kate is a 30-something Australian who had almost no sailing experience before meeting Hugh. While working as a project manager and juggling two boys she wrote this story as a record of their sailing adventure. Kate and Hugh have aspirations to go sailing again and to take their boys while they are still young for a life-shaping experience and to create a new generation of adventure seekers.

Kate & Hugh aboard *Elizabeth Jane II*

@katemacready_writer

The Trip

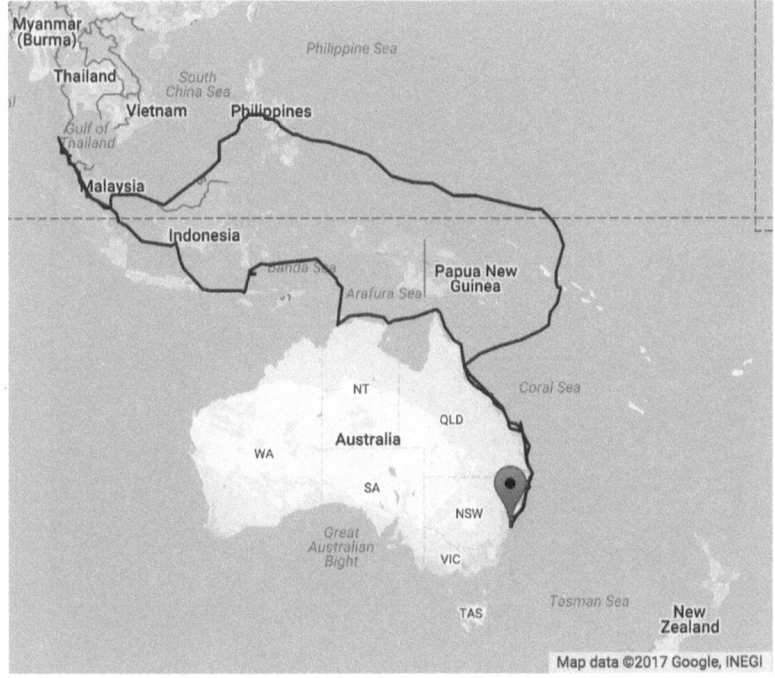

For Owen and Laurie, you mean the world to me.

CHAPTER ONE

We Come Here in Numbers

The show kicked off with one man in the centre of the empty field, he was wearing a skirt made from sewn canvas with simple sandals on his feet. He stood in front of the microphone and began to sing. The man belted out a battle cry, his strong voice calling his warriors to battle with him to protect their land from invaders. It was the story of the clan and the trials they experienced before Indonesia was a single nation, being a group of islands that lived isolated except for marriage, trade and as we were learning, war.

The group of twenty of us had been sat down as instructed by our guides in newly built bleachers that gave an unhindered view of the enormous field below. We were a ramshackle group of travellers who were sailing through Indonesia in a loosely organised group – a sailing rally. It was another scorching day with about 150% humidity; we were thankful for the shade above us. The dusty ground below was the size of about four soccer fields and we could see people dressed in long sleeved tops and pants of a bright red, green or blue and grouped together according to the colour of their outfits. Even from this distance we could see they were nervous, bouncing from one leg to the other. We had learnt from the previous experiences with our generous hosts that whatever we thought was going to happen was often a complete underestimation – and we waited excitedly trying to absorb what we could see.

Our fresh-faced guides Rakmi and Indah were next to us, silent and waiting to be spoken to. The two girls were very reserved and looked to be about 12 years old, though they told us they were 18 years old and were honoured to be our translators. Sweet, yet timid, their excitement at escorting us to the event was palpable. They were immaculately dressed with not a strand of hair protruding from under their hijabs. I was amazed at how well presented they were given the unrelenting heat which beat down. However, while their English was good, there were still lots of gaps to fill with hand gestures and charades.

"So what's happening?" asked Hugh, in the way I'd seen him open up a conversation over the years.

"The local schools practise for months," Rakmi said. "Today is first time together to dance."

"They haven't practised together?" he continued.

"No, too many people and live far away. They do groups of five hundred people and here will be twelve thousand." Rakmi said.

"Twelve thousand people?" Hugh asked wide-eyed turning to looking at me. "I can't believe that twelve thousand people are doing an organised dance for us! And who are we, just a bunch of visiting sailors on a group trip?" he turned back to Rakmi. "And who's this?"

"Oh the Sultan of Buton," Rakmi answered. "He is highest ruler."

The Sultan of Buton took his seat looking very regal in the stand next to us. He was dressed in an elaborately patterned sarong skirt with shirt atop - which Rakmi explained was called a *bodo gesung*. Seeing such an important person for the province - who before independence was the traditional ruler of the region, attending this performance increased our feelings of anticipation. On a platform below us the local TV newsreader started delivering her opening speech for camera and we could see that the whole performance would be recorded for telecast.

The lone man finished his beckoning cry to his tribe. A line of men beat sticks on drums draped around their necks, beating in unison as a signal. The song gave way to a battle scene where thousands of boys swarmed the field - mock war with sticks that you could hear cracking against each other from high up in the stands. We were riveted by the dance that told the history of the island: war, to religion, to food cultivation and work. Music pumped through loud speakers located throughout the field and grandstand; the tension rose and fell with the tone and pace of the songs, a mixture of traditional music and more contemporary versions of folklore songs. Each part of the story was told by groups of dancers who moved in from the side of the field and moved back as the next scene started. They danced using all of their bodies with the drum beat pulsating through them, we could see the joy on their faces as they were presenting their masterpiece.

The penultimate piece told the mythical story of a woman abused by her jealous fisherman husband. The voice of an angel reverberated around the field sending goose bumps up my spine. The woman and her husband stood alone and she cried out telling the story of him casting her out to sea. The song then moved to a brighter tone, more dancers entered the field and whipped coloured ribbons of blue around the woman as she rose from the ocean to be born again as the most beautiful mermaid who lived a joyful life under the sea. She was finally free of the torment of her marriage and lived in harmony with the fish and the waves. One day her husband came in his boat to beg her for mercy, to come back to him, but she rejected him and dove deeper under the ribbon waves. She was gone. Gone to sing her melodious song which we could hear as she disappeared. Tears rolled down our faces as we jumped up and clapped her as she left the field; the lingering sound of her song replaying in our ears.

The dance went for two hours and the dancers' enthusiasm could be felt from where we sat. The performance was reaching a climax as the twelve thousand dancers moved onto the field to do one final choreographed piece. This scene was the story of our visit and a humbling tribute to the pleasure our hosts derived from putting on a show like this. The dancers expressed the hope that this performance would be one of many with more tourists to come. Because they were standing in lines we could count that there were in fact twelve thousand people performing. It took our breath away. The masses remained on the field dancing and stomping to the beat from the music. *Takawa Kolossal* dance was literally: *Takawa* – 'We come here', *Kolossal* – 'in numbers'.

Rakmi and Indah grabbed our hands and pulled us up from our seats.
"Where are we going?" I asked.
"To see dancers. They so excited to see you." said Indah.

They led us and the others down the long stairs to the field where we were immediately mobbed by the crowd, just us and thousands of excited locals. It was overwhelming. They wanted to touch us, to dance with us, hold our hands and take photos together. It was something I had never experienced before giving me a glimpse into the lives of famous celebrities. We danced and laughed and took photos. All around we sensed the relief and exhilaration from the crowd that had completed their work and could now celebrate.

Soon the crowds became too much and our guides carefully shepherded us back to the waiting cars. We sighed as we sat back into the seats barely able to comprehend the events of the day. Such an immense performance.

It was a very unusual feeling to be driven around; to be led from place to place without having to think about what to do next. The motorcade zoomed through the streets and we absorbed the simple life that the people here lived. Houses with dirt floors, concrete walls and flimsy tin rooves. Yet, technology was ever present, televisions, the internet and phones. Everywhere we turned people were snapping pictures of us with their mobile phones. Thrusting their children at us to take a photo of the visiting 'celebrities' holding their children.
Rakmi and Indah were keen to help us.

"Do you need somethings?" Indah asked.

I thought for a second, "Oh, we need some milk."

"What is milk?" Indah and Rakmi looked at each other quizzically and thought for a while but couldn't remember the translation.

I sat in silence thinking what else I could use to answer the question. Then it came to me. "From cow, you know, moo moo."

They laughed "Ohhh, susu. Yes, susu. Okay, we find some, in town."

It's hard to imagine how we ended up here when only four months ago we were in Sydney and haphazardly pulling together our departure.

CHAPTER TWO

Leaving

"Oh my god, what have I done?" muttered Hugh under his breath as he watched me hanging on with white knuckles to the boat toe-rails and throwing up again overboard. "Is this the worst decision we ever made?"

Just an hour before we had been standing on the dock of the marina with oppressive grey clouds and heavy rain forming the backdrop to our small foursome. It seemed like the least auspicious Tuesday imaginable, the day of our big departure from Sydney.

"Good luck son, be careful." said Hugh's Dad – Ric as he held him by the shoulders and pulled him in for a hug, an unusual sign of physical affection.

"Of course Dad." said Hugh.

"Just be sensible." said Ric.

Hugh nodded and turned to our friend Krissy. "Thanks for coming Krissy, we can't wait for you to visit us in a few weeks."

"I don't really have any words. I'm gonna miss you two." she said as her and Hugh quickly exchanged a hug before walking over to me.

We didn't say anything, but hugged for a while. I was going to miss Krissy terribly too. We had been such good friends at work and had spent almost every weekend of the previous year together as we struggled to learn how to sail on a friend's boat.

"You've got the bottles for sending me messages?" she asked.

We stepped apart. I grinned and nodded, scared to say anything in case my voice gave away how nervous I was feeling. With one last look behind and a quick wave I stepped onto the boat after Hugh, while Krissy and Ric passed us the lines from the dock cleats and helped push us off.

This was our day of grand departure, pushing off the dock in our 44-foot sailing boat, a Peterson 44 – named *Elizabeth Jane II*. The boat that would be our home for the next, well, who knew; at least a year. We made our way out of the slip before hoisting the main sail. As I stood on the bow I could see Krissy and Ric becoming smaller at the dock as we drifted off, I waved an enthusiastic goodbye as tiny droplets of rain fell around us. I felt the butterflies of anticipation and some anxiety driven nausea, was this really a good idea? I busied myself with tidying the ropes on the deck and putting away the docklines to distract myself from these emotions. The wind was unpredictable but the sail filled and we slowly floated under the Sydney Harbour Bridge. For the first time we felt a feeling that would come back to us over and over again, that we were a small boat dwarfed by the enormity of the world around it.

I started thinking back to the busyness of the recent weeks while we got the boat ready for departure. Hugh had installed a new hand-pump toilet after he accidently dropped and smashed the old one on the dock while cleaning it. We'd had the boat dry-docked for a thorough bottom clean and checked the rigging which required replacement of two of the forestays. And while Hugh was busy with the boat work, I had been scouring the internet for information on things like what food to pack, figuring out what would fit and how to improve the lifespan of fresh food because our fridge was about half the size of a bar fridge. To make sure that we had as much fresh food as possible, I used 'ye olde' tricks that my grandmother might have used; putting potatoes in a dark coloured cotton bag and keeping them tucked away in a draw – away from onions and bananas, wrapping the tomatoes in paper before putting them in the fridge to extend their life. It also meant buying flour and spices and canned beans and saying no to pre-prepared foods that we didn't have the budget for. While I loved cooking, it was going to be a real test to make everything from scratch. I also went shopping for our on-board first aid kit which needed to include antibiotics, pain killers – strong ones, bandages, instant ice packs, burn creams, all the sorts of things we might need if we had to try and treat ourselves while at sea or in a remote location away from medical help. I learnt about what to take by reading blogs, websites and speaking with our doctor and hoped that we wouldn't have to use any of the items.

All of the prep work distracted us from comprehending the emotional challenges that lay ahead. We had never gone out in the open ocean together, we had barely been dating for a year and I had never sailed on a boat overnight – I had very little sailing experience at all for that matter. It sounded like a disaster waiting to happen. A familiar story of dreamers who were ill-prepared and sailed off into the sunset only to find that they got scared when the weather got rough or that they had run aground. Hugh got me through these fears with his confidence and bluster telling me that everything would be alright. Ignorance and hope fueled our hastily put together plan. With no route to follow or destination in mind we were to leave Sydney and head north - literally seeing where the wind took us. I suppose we had taken the 'planning and sailing don't mix' mantra to heart. There were so many variables that scheduling what you would do in great detail was a sure-fire way to set yourself up for failure. So we had gone to the other extreme, with no end point, no target destination, we were just sailing to see how far we could get.

And it was during this short time before our departure that we lived at the marina in Woolwich in Sydney. We met some wonderful other cruisers who had years more experience and really brought us up to speed with the essentials - they gave us our first glimpse into the lifestyle and what people were like who lived on the water. These inspiring people had sailed many oceans, like crossing from the United States to Australia through the Pacific and other Australians who had done it all before. 'Cruisers' was a term we would come to embrace – a term used for people who lived on their boats for leisure and slowly made their way from place to place, this was in stark contrast to racing sailors or people who worked on boats.

Jake and Jackie were an upbeat and positive couple from the US, they were very excited about sailing and we met them on our first day at Woolwich marina. One key moment that sticks out for me was when we told them that Hugh had accidentally dropped and smashed the ceramic toilet, Jake said "well, there's no coming back from that", summing up the situation in his typical dry way. Jake was about five foot ten, skinny as a rake and was tanned like leather, with a sunglass tan line etched into his face. He had dark brown hair and crease lines around his eyes and mouth from his infectious smile. Jake was so full of life and loved the sea, surfing and had a keen obsession with scuba diving, a pursuit he would inspire Hugh to take up as we sailed together. Jake and Hugh got on like a house on fire, they shared an interest in the technical aspects of sailing, navigation and the ins and outs of diesel boat engine workings.

Jackie was more reserved, but she always welcomed you with her warm southern accent with a "how y'all doin'?" and a broad smile. I felt like we had more in common, she had not been a sailor, but had become one to accompany her husband on his dream of circumnavigating the world. You could tell she didn't quite feel completely relaxed on the boat, but had made it home with plush cushions and beautiful mementoes from the places they had been. It was a great ocean-going boat and they looked after it like it was their first born. Their boat was immaculate. A friend we made later – Zdenka, told a story about how when Jake and Jackie arrived in the Bundaberg marina and were being cleared in by Australian customs officials, the officials called their boat - *Hokulea* the 'cleanest boat in the Pacific' because there was not a rope out of place or speck of dirt to be found anywhere. They were meticulous about keeping the boat clean, tidy and in the best working order. Jackie loved hosting and we were frequently invited over for sundowner drinks and nibbles. The two were seasoned cruisers who had sailed from California and spent two years crossing the Pacific Ocean before we had met them at the marina. One night in Sydney aboard their boat we gleaned detailed information from the experienced pair. It was from Jake and Jackie that we learned about seasickness tablets – because Jackie was horribly afflicted, anchoring techniques and the community on the High Frequency radio – known as the cruisers net. This radio network of hundreds of people would become a crucial component of our lives and we would befriend other cruisers over the airwaves.

The sailing people we met in Sydney would stay close friends of ours throughout the trip and we would even sail together at times.

I was lingering on folding the docklines as we slowly made our way up the harbour and turned back for one last glimpse of the landmark buildings of the Sydney skyline and the Opera House before we refocused our attention on our big exit out the Sydney Heads. The swell of the crossing waters of the harbour and the Pacific Ocean at the opening of the Sydney Heads was like a washing machine and we bumped and swayed and made our way through in an ugly fashion. The noise of the boat in the water was something I was unprepared for, the banging of the boom as the unsteady nature of the boat in the water meant it moved with the swaying, items rolling around down in the cabin that we had not tied down adequately, waves crashing into the side of the hull and the sounds of the water crashing into the shore. This was not the comfortable, relaxing sailing experience I had signed up for. As a green pallor took over my face I looked longingly at the shore behind us and wished for solid, steady ground. I looked into Hugh's eyes and could see the doubt wash over his face. In my eyes he could see a flash of regret as we gave away our comfortable land-lubbing life for one on a boat.

As we entered the Pacific Ocean waters and turned the boat north to make for the Central Coast a few glimmers of sunshine peaked through the dense clouds and warmed my face. It was all I could enjoy as the ocean-going was not treating me well. While the conditions were quite mild it became apparent to me that I was not well adapted to the swell and waves of the ocean. I knew that I was prone to seasickness but I had hoped that I could overcome my biological weakness to become acclimatised to sailing. I could hope right?

Hugh thankfully single-handedly managed all the sailing with ease. The sailing came as second nature to him as he had been doing amateur racing on boats for almost 20 years. He was pleased that some wind had come up from the south and he unfurled our big jib sail to capture the freshening breeze which gave us a push while we slowly made progress on our short first sail. He gave me a pat on the hand as I lurched away while my stomach churned again. We made our miles north, they went by slowly and the sailing itself was unremarkable.

Late in the day Hugh went down to the cabin below and re-emerged with what became our trusty sailing guide for the Australian east coast. He flicked through the book and started reading aloud. "'The calming waters of the Pittwater Bay provide safe harbour to the sailor who is struggling against unfavourable conditions either heading north or south. It also offers an almost limitless number of secluded bays and anchorages for the day sailor'. Well, that sounds like an invitation for us," he remarked, "secluded bays are just what the seasick first mate ordered." Hugh continued to flick through the book to find some anchorage options. "Ah, here." he said. "'America Bay, the finest anchorage in the world'." Hugh snorted, "Well that sounds like some writer's liberty right there. The finest anchorage in the world? We might just have to check it out. What do you think?"

"Sure, whatever. Just make the boat stop." I moaned.

"That sounds like concurrence from the first mate. Let's go." Hugh said heartily to the imaginary broader crew as he stood behind the wheel of the boat and prepared to turn into the Bay.

The change in the swell was almost instantaneous as we turned into the Bay and away from the choppy seas of the open ocean. The swell disappeared, the noise quietened and we glided into the enormous and wide bay. My seasickness finally abated and I was able to enjoy the view of the golden yellow sands that hugged the coast dominated by hills covered in dense green foliage – gum trees and any combination of shrubs and other small natives. This National Park north of Sydney had always been somewhere that I enjoyed and now we could anchor at its edge and truly soak up the sounds and life of the bush.

After an hour of navigating into the quiet waterway, Hugh dropped the anchor with the chain clinking link after link through the bow roller until the anchor thudded to the sandy floor below. And for the first time in ten hours, there was silence. No noise from the boat banging and clanging along, no waves bumping into the side of the boat. It was just us in a tiny secluded bay – America Bay. There was something special about the place, the soft sound of the waterfall, the tree lined cliffs around the bay, the brilliant sunset combined with enjoying a delicious boat-made chicken stroganoff for dinner. It was a fine end to our first sail which had been anything from smooth.

All the hard work and preparation had paid off, we had thrown off the doubts and trepidation. We had left.

CHAPTER THREE

In The Beginning

We ended up spending the next few days sailing and relaxing in the calm waters of Pittwater, just north of Sydney. It was during this time that I reflected on the previous nine months where this crazy idea of a sailing trip had been born during an off-hand discussion Hugh and I had while drinking a bottle of wine after another lousy day at work. I was sick of pushing paper through bureaucratic hoops while Hugh was bored from the lack of technological innovation his work offered him. I had been working on complex infrastructure projects for the government while Hugh was an engineer for a multinational company building tele-communication networks. We had been reading a book about a couple who had gone off sailing around the world with no experience or understanding of what they were in for. That got us talking.

"Could you imagine if we had a boat and sailed the world?" I asked.

"Sure, I mean, you know it's been a dream of mine since I was a teenager." said Hugh as his eyes lit up.

"But how do you go from being a lazy Sunday sailor - like me - to someone who conquers oceans?" I asked.

Hugh scratched the stubble on his chin as he pondered the question.

The first thing you notice about Hugh is his height, he is tall, taller than most people, he stands at almost two metres and is used to bending his neck and head slightly to the side to hear what people around him are saying. He has broad shoulders and stands tall when not leaning in to speak or shake hands with someone. His brown hair curls when it grows long and into a fluffy afro which he hates, so he keeps it cut. His sideburns are a dull orange and frame his face which lights up when he smiles. While he is 32, people often mistake him for being at least five years older - I think his height contributes to that appearance of maturity, combined with his slightly sun weathered face and his air of confidence.

"Well I have done a fair bit of off-shore racing and I can show you." said Hugh, taking another sip of wine.

To me this was just one of the many random conversations that we had, but Hugh took this conversation to be my approval of the idea and he immediately started scanning the internet looking at boats for sale and seeing how much they cost. Surely we could not afford a boat, only rich people go sailing right? Hugh took on the boat research as a part time job and was shortlisting various designs that were suitable for ocean sailing and fitted our very limited budget. In a matter of weeks he had found one online that suited– a 44-foot cruising yacht, built 34 years ago by the US boat designing pair Jack Kelly and Doug Peterson, for sale in Sydney after being sailed here from the USA. The model was called a Peterson 44 and had a very good reputation for ocean sailing, this particular boat had already crossed at least the Pacific Ocean to get to Australia. It also had all the kit for ocean sailing with extra anchors, spare sails and heavy weather gear for rough conditions. The seller was keen to sell as they were moving overseas and needed the money quickly, this meant they had open ears to some tough bargaining by Hugh.

The boat was in Sydney and easy to visit one sunny Saturday. I didn't know what I was looking at, as I had only been on very small sailing boats for Sunday racing a handful of times. A cruising boat is a whole different class of vessel because it has living spaces below, comfortable beds, a galley - kitchen, a head – toilet and shower, things most racing boats don't have because people don't live on them, at least not for more than a week or so. But Hugh was in his element, he was looking the boat all over, checking the rigging, the sailing gear, the sails, the electronic instruments, he was sold on this boat from the moment he saw it. At this point I had really handed over the decision making to Hugh and he started to negotiate with the boat broker on a price. And before we knew it the seller had accepted our offer. In under an hour we were boat owners! Over the course of the next fortnight we paid the deposit and hauled the boat out onto a dry dock so that a qualified boat surveyor could check the structure for us to see if it was still watertight and a good investment. He gave it the big tick and now there was no stopping us, the settlement would proceed. By making these decisions we were on our way to our grand ocean adventure – after all, there's no point owning a boat if you are not going to use it.

We then started looking at our belongings and sorting them into piles of things to sell, things to give away, things to put on the boat and some things to put in storage for use on our return. Everything had to be culled, dramatically. I decided to sell my house and Hugh gave his housemate notice that he would be leaving. We used websites to sell our cars and some belongings, and put all of the money into our sailing kitty. I am not a person who is attached to many physical belongings, so it became refreshing and liberating to be free of furniture and other things - to let it all go. We had to be very selective about what we would keep in storage as it was an expense that we would have to pay out of our savings. So we whittled it down to key furniture items like a fridge, two beds, a washing machine, a dining table and chairs, my grandmother's pianola and some kitchenware. This all fitted in half a single carspace garage. In the end, this was the sum of mine and Hugh's belongings and the basic things we thought would be useful for starting our lives again on our return.

While I was quite detached from the realisation of what we were doing, we were committing to the sailing trip idea more and more each day as we changed our life. We were cutting our ties from our comfortable and predictable life where we had a regular paycheck, friends, and homes that were safe and stable on land. But I continued to have this underlying feeling of doubt wondering if Hugh and I should do this together, if we were even right for such an adventure. I was also worried about whether I could make it, whether I could survive on a boat. I literally had no idea what I was getting myself into and I began to realise that only by living it would I find out. So that was what propelled the leap of faith, the leap into the unknown. It was an exciting and frightening idea at the same time.

One that was attracting me like a magnetic force that I couldn't seem to break. I had to try this and fail or succeed before I could turn away from it.

I come from a family who have not spent time with boats, the predictable response from my parents when we told them what we were planning was shock and they thought I was mad. Dad in particular was convinced that I would die. "You are going to what?!" he exclaimed.
"Come on Dad. It'll be fine, we will be careful. It's just a different way of travelling." I said.
I am sure that visions of sailing disaster movies or mad people on remote islands like in the movie 'Castaway' flickered through my Dad's mind as he looked gravely at me. "You don't even know how to sail…" his voice trailed off as he looked away, he couldn't form the words to explain this fear he had about the whole idea.
My Mum came over "Your Dad is very worried about you, you know."
I just shrugged, there was nothing I could do. But thankfully Hugh stepped in "we will be very careful, I have spent a lot of time learning about the weather, we won't take stupid risks. Plus I have been offshore sailing many times before." He looked at my Dad to see if anything was resonating and continued, "our boat is very strong, it has a very good ocean-going reputation, it is 30 years old after all."

Dads face was softening as he was listening to Hugh's commonsense, I knew that he just needed some rational words to help calm him down.

Hugh's family was more upbeat, they had seen this side of Hugh before. It was in fact Hugh's Dad who had planted this seed of crazy adventures deep in Hugh's makeup. When he was just 16, Hugh and his Dad flew a small twin engine plane from Sydney around the world. Just the two of them. At such a formative age, this experience shaped Hugh and made him continually search for something new and challenging to aspire to, each adventure grander than the last. Hugh is a romantic and spends much time dreaming about far-fetched ideas – after all, it was he who came up with the idea for the trip. He is an adventurer with no limit to his imagination. Hugh had also spent a few years working for the UN doing work to restore communications in disaster zones, he was a first responder and yearned for the excitement and challenge that living a different life offered.

So his family just nodded and were unsurprised by the latest fantastic proposal Hugh had come up with. Our friends all thought it was terribly romantic, visions of a hazy long sunset on a tropical island formed their view of the adventure. They would all comment on how much they would love to do something like that, but, but…any excuse, and that was the real challenge, leaving. Lots of people talk about cutting free from the mundane city life of working and commuting only able to fantasise about leaving their normal life. But few actually do it. This was the scary part, quitting jobs, secure, comfortable, well-paying jobs to go and, what? Live on a boat, a caravan on the sea? The fear of the unknown was overwhelming. I had visions that the trip would only last a few weeks before we would call it quits. I was worried that our relationship wouldn't stand up to the challenge, that I would hate the sea, the isolation, that my sea sickness would be insurmountable, that I would miss the comforts of land-life. There were so many unknowns, but we had come too far to turn back now.

We never really spoke to our work colleagues about the trip. We ended up just resigning shortly ahead of our planned departure. There was something about saying "we are going away, on a boat and we don't quite know where to, or when we will be back." It was a commitment; something final. If I was talking about it at work it was something I would have to follow through with, I suppose deep down I was hoping that there would be something outside my control that would cause the whole plan to fall apart and we wouldn't have to leave.

Some people spend years getting ready for a trip like ours and some get so caught up in preparing to go that they never leave. It was just over six months from buying the boat to us leaving. We were motivated to get going, to see the world and not become rusted at the dock. We knew that this was just the beginning.

CHAPTER FOUR

Getting into our Sailing Groove

I had wonderful mental images of the east coast of Queensland. Long golden beaches, bathed in glorious sunshine all year round. It was about two months since we left Sydney and we arrived in the Whitsundays, fabled for having magnificent sailing conditions and being in a word – 'perfect'. But the reality of our north-bound sailing leg was far from that. The wind was howling, often blowing 30 knots and the skies were angry and overcast.

In the time since we left Sydney we were slowly getting into the groove of the sailing lifestyle. We had been fixing small problems on the boat, bush walking on uninhabited islands and buying fresh seafood from coastal fish co-ops. We had started tuning into the cruisers radio net which was a scheduled dial in at the same time every day over the HF radio. The radio frequency changed slightly depending on our location. We could communicate with boats up to 2000 miles away, and we were champing at the bit to hear what the other cruisers had to say about anchorages or conditions to expect further up the coast. It was a link for us to the sailing community as we rarely got to meet any people in real life. The group was a random collection of people who were sailing north, roughly to Darwin, and we also got to follow the progress of the cruising friends we had met in Sydney. Many of the people on the net were circumnavigators who were sailing through Australia as part of their world-journey. We learned that we were at the back of the pack as the other boats were further north of us, this meant that we got to savour all their tips which added some more up-to-date detail to our cruising guide.

The voices we heard over the radio each morning provided advice about good anchorages or where to buy delicious local food as well as warnings about sailing hazards. We did learn that one of our cruising friends from Sydney - Bill would be in the Whitsundays at the same time as we would be. So we hatched a plan to meet up with him. Hugh and I were desperate for some other company after just talking to each other for the last two months. We had also loosely arranged months back when we were still in Sydney for

Krissy to come and join us for a week aboard and keep us company, and the Whitsundays offered the perfect island-hopping destination for her to soak up the cruising lifestyle.

Hamilton Island was the rendezvous point. The bars, food and fancy resort activities on offer provided an interesting contrast to the abundance of nature that we had been submerged in on our slow sailing dawdle. Suddenly we were propelled into a world of motor boats, resort golf carts and swim up bars. Krissy flew in to meet us and we caught up to Bill who had been sailing ahead of us until now. We planned to do a few days tootling around the Whitsundays and enjoying the famous beauty and waterways of the area.

It was five months ago when we had met Bill at the marina in Sydney, a single-handed sailor who had made the two-year Pacific Ocean crossing. Bill was in his late 40s, a tall and lean guy with a thick mop of blond hair peppered with white in contrast to his bronzed skin. He had a laugh that you could hear from across the room and he often finished with a snort which usually started off another round of laughing. He was a social guy who loved to meet new people and it was a strange juxtaposition because he was a solo sailor and spent so much time alone at sea. It takes a special person to be a solo sailor – known as single handed sailors, one had to enjoy their own company for up to weeks at a time. Bill was friendly and affectionate, always hugging you around the shoulders; friendship meant a lot to him. He loved poetry and writing and trying to capture moments with his still camera. His character was personified in the work that he did as a professional cameraman - he had worked on countless Hollywood movies and it was as though he was looking at every experience through a lens, trying to tell the most captivating story.

It was great to welcome Krissy to tropical paradise, though it didn't feel much like paradise with the miserable weather and sailing conditions. It turns out that June is definitely not the time of year to visit the isles and we suffered one uncomfortable anchorage after another.
"Krissy!" I yelled and started running towards her as she hopped off the airport shuttle bus next to the marina.
"Kate!" she responded and dropped her bags as I came in for a hug.
She stepped back and looked at me "you're so tanned. I didn't know what I would find when I saw you two, maybe you would be all skinny and crazy from being away from land." she said.
"We haven't been gone that long!" I said.
"It's so great to see you, have I got some treats for you." she said as she opened up her bag to show off chocolate biscuits, fresh meat and lollies.
"You're the best!" I said, unable to look away from the goodies in her bag. "Come and jump aboard and put your

bags down, we should go get some lunch with Bill, he's here too."

"Bill's here? Awesome!" said Krissy.

Krissy is so bubbly and full of life that nothing seems to bother her and any sailing challenge makes the experience that much more interesting, she was always up for an adventure. She and I had spent a couple of winter seasons sailing a friend's 7m long racing boat on Sydney harbour in the weekly competition. It was an introduction to sailing for both of us, and we had bonded over our lack of skill and awkwardness on boats.

Over the next week Krissy, Hugh and I slowly moved from one anchorage to another in the Whitsunday island group, snorkelling, exploring the islands on foot and relaxing aboard. It was special to spend this time soaking up the area with her, reminding us again that experiences are for sharing and that this time together would be our last for a long while.

On the second last day Krissy was aboard with us, we sailed to Airlie Beach. The wind was cranking and we sailed in with 30 knots rocketing us toward the mainland harbour. Bill was also sailing the same route and we had fun taking photos of each other's boats. He photographed us under sail and was one of our favourite shots of the boat with white water licking the bow of the boat and the sails reefed in tight due to the strong wind. It proved that Hugh had done a good job of selecting a good ocean-going boat that could handle the more challenging conditions. It didn't feel much like fun to me at the time because my seasickness had lingered - I was busy hunkering down in the cockpit trying unsuccessfully to get it to abate. The time with Krissy on the boat was fun and it was nice to spend time with someone from home, someone we felt familiar with. We were constantly meeting new people but we craved that deeper relationship and connection we had with people from home. This was a feeling that would return to us over and over again throughout our time away. I suppose that people who travel via any means feel the same emotion, it doesn't matter whether you are away for work or a holiday, any extended period can make you crave home, feel homesick and miss friends. The next day she flew back to Sydney, it would be almost two years until we saw Krissy again.

We had decided over beers at a bar in Airlie Beach one night that we would sail to Darwin in company with Bill and then think about where to go from there. For the other northbound legs we shared some meals aboard with Bill and he caught us up on some great anchorages that he had been to on his way north from Sydney that we had skipped past. Hugh was careful to take notes so that he could use this information later when we were next in those locations. Bill was keen to show off his newfound crabbing skills, so we were on the lookout for good crabbing locations, muddy water next to mangroves were the fertile places we were looking for. It was in Magnetic Island that Bill caught a big crab.

"Yahoo, a bluey!" cried Bill, as he hoisted up his trap to find one miserable looking blue swimmer crab staring back at him, displeased at being captive.

"Awesome work Bill." said Hugh.

"I love crabs," said Bill, "have you ever had a fresh one?" he asked Hugh.

"Nah mate, never been lucky enough." said Hugh.

"Well you are in for a treat, I'll show you what I do." he said. The three of us took the dingy the short distance back to his boat '*Solstice*'. I was careful to sit at the opposite end of the dingy to the crab who was anxiously sticking his claw through the trap bars for something to snap at. Back at the boat Bill showed Hugh how he tipped the crab out of the trap into a big bucket full of sea water.

"What, you're not going to kill it?" I asked.

"No, Katie, you kill them right before you cook em. I keep em in this bucket until then. We should have it tonight for dinner, it's not very big for three, but it'll still be delicious." said Bill.

"Sounds great. You just have to hope that he doesn't go on an adventure in your boat while we are out ey Bill?" said Hugh.

Bill snorted, "Ey, Ey. Yeah, no crabs on the loose!"

Later that night Bill killed, gutted and boiled up the crab and served it with a rich garlic butter sauce. It was magic, the crab meat was so sweet and delicate. We indulged in the freshest crab we would ever eat straight from the ocean to the plate. This was the kind of experience that keeps people out cruising for such a long time, having access to amazingly fresh food is rarely experienced in city life.

The sail up the east coast of Queensland was dominated by cargo ships and reef dodging. The Great Barrier Reef hugged the coast line with a thin strip of clear waterway separating the two, where our slow sailing boats had to share the passage with the large cargo and mining ships steaming alongside. The overnight passages were dominated by looking around with eagle eyes to spot the shipping traffic and listening out on the radio for their calls to discuss navigation if they were passing us. Their voices made for a refreshing change to the otherwise lonely and monotonous sailing night shifts we were doing. We did as many short sailing legs as we could, breaking them down into single overnight or day sails. But this became harder the further north we went as anchorages became harder to find. The Queensland coast became our training ground for learning the things we needed to do on the longer passages, like the two or three day trips we found ourselves in the more remote parts of Australia's top end.

The longer sailing legs were a steep learning curve for both of us and it brought us closer together. Spending so much time with one person in a confined space was a unique challenge for both of us and we had to rely on each other 100 percent, look after each other and spend the effort to give back to each other. The time on the water was solitary, at times lonely and we had to look after each other for support. We got to know each other better, by reading body language and facial expressions we could tell if the other was tired or didn't want to talk. We had to respect what the other needed, give them the time and space to come back replenished from within.

It was a bit over three months after we departed Sydney that we arrived in Darwin to find ourselves in the middle of a big cruisers meet up, there was something like 100 boats converged in one port. There were three rallies leaving Darwin around the same time that would take the cruisers to different destinations in Papua New Guinea or Indonesia. We had decided just days before to join one of them – the Sail Indonesia Rally. It was here in this busy anchorage that we finally got to put some faces to the names and voices of people we had been listening to over the net for the last three months. Jack was in his fifties with a grey head of hair and the typical cruiser sun tanned skin. When he smiled his whole face lit up and when he laughed, his body laughed too. He and his wife Zdenka were a warm and fun couple who had so far navigated half the world sailing from Maine on the east coast of the United States over the previous three years. Zdenka had dark brown hair streaked with grey which she kept cut short. She too had the customary cruiser tan and wore her sunglasses around her neck on a chain, wise from the experience of losing glasses overboard. She carried the New Yorker accent, though it wasn't as sharp as Jack's and perhaps that was because she had lived in Europe for the first part of her life.

We had actually listened to Jack and Zdenka on the cruisers radio – the net, for months while sailing the east coast of Australia before finally meeting them in person in Darwin. Their voices permeated our cabin in the mornings and seemed like part of our regular ritual as we would routinely check-in and hear what the other cruisers had to say about conditions or anchoring location recommendations, it was almost like radio personalities who became part of your household, you would listen to them everyday and you felt like they were truly a part of your lives, when really it is a long distance relationship with someone you may never meet in person.

"So I have to introduce you to our friends Jack and Zdenka," said Bill "they've sailed here from the US, we met in Fiji."

"Yeah, g'day," said Hugh, "we feel like we already know you, we have been listening to you on the net for months now. It's nice to meet you in person." He stuck out his hand and shook Jack and then Zdenka's hand.

"Ha, yeah, that's so weird that you can talk to people for ages over the radio when you're a cruiser. You meet them and you feel like you already know each other, but you've never actually met. That strange moment of matching the voice to the face!" said Zdenka.

"So you guys are Aussies huh?" asked Jack.

"Yeah, from Sydney, but we're going to do the Indo Rally." said Hugh.

"'Indo', you guys always shorten words, it's something that strikes me about you Ozzies." said Jack with a laugh.

"Don't want to waste too much time talking now." said Hugh jokingly.

"We're doing the rally too. We decided to do the eastern route. It's more sailing, but going the southern route would be a bit busy, so many boats going that way." said Jack.

"Hmm, yeah. We haven't decided which route to take yet, maybe we should talk more about the stops hey. Can I buy you guys a beer?" Hugh asked.

We did not know it at the time, but meeting these two would be the start of a special relationship that would carry through our time sailing in Asia.

CHAPTER FIVE

New Shores

We could smell Saumlaki before we saw it. The combination of fragrances made our noses tickle, with the smells emanating from drying herbs and dense wood smoke making me cough lightly. It was a pitch-black night and our anticipation of arriving somewhere new, somewhere that was not Australia, kept us alert and excited while we carefully entered the dark harbour at 2am. It was strange to think we had been in Australia just three days earlier preparing to sail into a new country.

After seeing some of Australia's most remote coastline through far north Queensland and the Northern Territory we had made it to Darwin and enjoyed being back in a busy city again. We got to work tidying up the boat to get her ready for our leap into international waters. It was only a three-day journey to Saumlaki in Indonesia, but the symbolism of leaving behind what you know, your mother tongue and your familiar customs was a bigger emotional journey. And it was this time going through the northern Australian waters that we decided to join the Indonesian Sailing Rally, an event promoted by the Indonesian tourism board which gathered together a group of boats and put them on a combined route, stopping at promoted destinations. We would be assisted by local guides when we arrived in port and it sounded like an easier way for us to see the more remote parts of Indonesia and manage the checking-in process along the way. Our friends Jack and Zdenka and Jake and Jackie were also going on the route and our three boats formed part of a group of 12 others going on the northern rally route through Indonesia. It became quickly apparent to Hugh and I that we were by far the youngest in the group, with majority of the cruisers being much older and having spent decades planning their cruising retirement.

Leaving Sydney had felt like a monumental achievement, but as we struggled north along the east coast of Australia it started to pale in comparison. The powerful East Australian Current flows south and made our travels tiresome and plain hard work. Working our way through the Great Barrier Reef was challenging and frightening as we carefully dodged cargo ships while slowly navigating the narrow passages between the landform to our west and the reef to our east. This busy water highway offered little forgiveness for navigational errors. Rounding Cape York and stepping foot on land to pop a bottle of champagne atop Australia's northern-most tip was a wonderful reward for our northbound trek. Finally, we had conquered the east coast. The west bound leg to Darwin was downright miserable and the choppy seas of the Gulf of Carpentaria showed me that despite my highest hopes for overcoming seasickness I was only going to make it by taking medication. I was disappointed to give up on the dream of not getting seasick, but it seemed that that was where this hope belonged – as a dream. It had been hard on Hugh as he had been left doing most of the sailing work while I was moaning about being sick - I needed to be more help on deck. The downside was that the antihistamine in the medication made me feel very lethargic and sleepy: an inconvenient side effect for someone who is meant to be alert and able to respond to danger while sailing.

I felt a rush of excitement and butterflies in my stomach as we dropped anchor in Saumlaki in the darkness of the night, awaiting the new day and the new experiences. As we laid our head on our pillows we could hear the unmistakable tones of the pre-dawn call to prayer sounding out across the water. The feelings of leaving Australia and the world we knew started to feel a lot more real: the previous three days that we had spent crossing the sea between Darwin and Saumlaki had left us bruised and weary, as the sea was choppy with big swells and a strong wind. This had been our longest passage to date and it was out in the open ocean, not hugging the coast line as we had done for the previous three months since we had left Sydney. It felt like a big deal, I mean, we were just starting out so we didn't have anything to compare it to.

At 8am we woke to the VHF radio crackling and we were hailed by the local customs and immigration officials. Our first experience at checking-in to a new country was very interesting as they insisted on boarding our boat and checking through our belongings. It was like being at the airport where you are screened by customs, except this time instead of just having a bag scanned, you have your whole house checked over. Indonesia, like many countries, is very strict about what you can bring into their country. This includes medications, ones that include opioids – like codeine and oxycodone, and weapons – like guns. Some cruisers carry guns on their boats as a protection in the case of being boarded by thieves or pirates. We decided not to carry a gun, not least because we have not used them before, but also because we thought that they would escalate a hostile situation and might result in terrible injury, probably to us. So before being visited by customs we went through the process of hiding some of our serious pain medication that we stored in our first aid kit in case we needed it while at sea and once boarded, signed a declaration confirming we were not carrying a gun.

The officials that came to our boat to do the official checking-in procedure arrived in the most comical of ways. They didn't own boats themselves and so they had borrowed a local fisherman and his wooden boat - with an engine that made a loud putt-putt-putt-putt sound as it carved its way through the water to bring the officials over. After the fisherman's boat was tied up to ours, the five officials almost falling in the water, managed to clamber aboard our yacht. The first thing that struck me was their presentation, they were immaculately presented wearing different coloured uniforms depending on the departments they represented, either in full navy with shoulder lapels or black pants with a tan shirt. Whatever the colour combination, the pants had an ironed crease for an extra sharp appearance and a crisp ironed shirt with black leather shoes that were so shiny you could see your reflection. It was hard to tell who was representing what department and they all started asking for paperwork. But it became obvious that a couple of the entourage were just over for a sticky beak, as they walked up and down the foredeck of the boat or down in the cabin below to see our computers or stove, taking photos along the way. They spoke to each other in Bahasa Indonesian and used short two or three

English word combinations when asking for something from us.

"You have passport?" queried the officer. He looked like the boss man as he had the most stripes on his shoulder lapel.

"Yes, here they are and here are some copies, how many do you need?" asked Hugh. He waited for the men to respond, but their heads were buried in their paper folders, so he just counted them out with a few extra for good measure.

"Visa?" the officer continued.

Hugh flicked to the page in our passports and handed over more photocopies of that page.

"Boat papers?" asked another. This seemed to be our registration, so Hugh grabbed another handful of copies from our paper stash.

"Boat stamp? Where is boat stamp?" asked the boss.

Hugh and I looked at each other quizzically. We had heard some other cruisers talking about a boat stamp, but we didn't have one and didn't realise that it would be important. It usually just contains in text the boat name, registration number and captain's name so it can be stamped on sheets for the officials to witness Hugh's signature.

"We need boat stamp, where is stamp?" he started demanding.

"Ah, well, we do not have one. But I can fill it all in for you." said Hugh.

The boss man huffed and looked very put out. He started packing away his papers as if he was going to leave without finishing it at all. I looked at Hugh and he saw the panic in my eyes, we definitely needed our boat visa and passport stamped to confirm our entry, otherwise we would experience a world of bureaucratic pain at the ports after this one.

"No, no...," said Hugh, "I can fill in the sections, no problem, just a minute." Hugh delicately took the papers from the boss and started filling in the boat name, his name, the boat registration number and signed each one. It was a laborious task and he had to do it for about 40 papers. He managed to bring some humour to it as he completed writing all the details out, acted as though he had a stamp in his hand and was pressing it onto the sheet with a "wah-lah!" sound as he looked at the men with a smile on his face. This evoked a laugh from our visitors and seemed to calm what looked like a disastrous situation.

The men studied the papers in great detail and there were so many papers, it was a big job. Hugh continued filling in some forms of theirs and signing all manner of documents as the captain and master of the vessel. As Hugh was caught up with the work I was watching the men and I could see that they were not very comfortable on the boat, as it had developed a slight roll from the swell coming into the harbour. The boss man was looking worse with each roll of the boat and was turning a light shade of green.

"Whiskey?" one of the men asked Hugh.

Hugh was aware that the men might ask for a gift for doing our paperwork and he shook his head "no, no, maybe a soda drink?" Hugh asked the men "coke, sprite?".

The men didn't look surprised that we hadn't taken the bait and nodded. So I went down and picked up a few cans of sprite that we had on board and brought them back to the cockpit where they were all sitting and passed them around. The men drank them and started to look a little better after having some of the sugary drinks.

The whole experience took over one hour and as the minutes ticked by they became in a hurry to get off the boat and back onto stable land. In a flurry, the boss man provided our visa which lasted for 90 days and all of our clearing-in requirements were ticked off. They had to hail the fisherman to come back and collect them, so we watched as he noisily putted over in his wooden boat and the officials struggled to disembark without falling in the water.

Hugh and I stood on the side of the boat as the last man stepped onto the fisherman's boat and helped push them off, we used our limited Indonesian "terima kasih" to thank the men and wiped the sweat from our brow. We had formally checked-in to Indonesia, we were free to go to shore and experience the place.

We had packed away our day-to-day items for the passage, so it took a little while to get things together for a shore excursion. This required unloading and reinflating the dingy, attaching the outboard engine and hoisting them down to the water below. We packed our bags with money, camera and water and hopped in ourselves before slowly whirring our way towards shore a short distance from where we had anchored. As we drew nearer and could see a line of concrete buildings one street back from the shore and a colourful market closest to the pier that we were heading towards. We tied our dingy up to some steps on a concrete pier next to the customs office and walked out to find ourselves in the centre of a bustling, noisy and grimy port town.

I could see a market off to my right selling fresh food and meat and straight ahead a row of shops selling clothes, materials and household items like mops and buckets. The road was packed dirt and plumes of dust kicked up when locals on small motorbikes rode through. The air was filled with noise of motorbikes roaring, chatter, children laughing and large cargo ships hooting their horns. Around us kids were running in flimsy thongs wearing shorts and t-shirts emblazoned with English football team emblems. The kids were giggling, pointing and staring at Hugh, saying "Tinggi Man, Tinggi Man" which we later learnt meant 'tall man, tall man'.

It was unnerving, but we would slowly get used to the local people staring at us, something that would follow us for our entire time in Asia. I felt like I was watching a movie, the whole experience did not feel real to me and I was just soaking up what I saw. In the three days it had taken us to sail here I felt like we were a million miles from Australia with the life of the Indonesian people being so different from ours. Feeling a bit overwhelmed, we took a break and found a local street vendor who was selling nasi goreng – fried rice and a coke and we refueled after what had been an exhausting few days at sea.

While we sat eating the tasty rice and taking a rest from walking around, the smells that hit us as we had been sailing into the harbour that morning wafted over us again and I got up to follow the scent, intrigued by the sensory tingling it evoked in me. As I followed the smell I found myself wandering bent over through the ramshackle markets which comprised various brightly coloured tents which were loosely pegged to create awnings at about one and a half metres off the ground – far below my head height. The further in I went, the stronger the smell. Kids were pushing past me chasing their younger siblings or their chickens, on the loose. I wasn't paying attention to the vendors trying to sell me their produce as all I wanted to do was find this permeating smell that triggered the emotions within me of exploring a new land. I emerged from the maze of tents to find myself in a small clearing which was filled with dozens of tarpaulins stretched out on the ground and covered in small brown things and spread out thinly so it was only one layer thick. The midday sun was beaming as I bent down to look closer to see what they were. Then I realised it was the spices - cloves, star anise, nutmeg all laid out. They had just been picked and were being dried in the sun for packaging and sale at the markets.

The women tending them walked around me spreading the spices out with a rake to make sure they were not overlapping each other. We learned later that the women would bring them in each night and lay them out again the next day to ensure that they did not get wet if it rained overnight. It was a laborious task, but one which the people around this area had been doing for hundreds of years. We were approaching the fabled spice islands, steeped in history as a land that the British, the Dutch and the Portuguese had had bloody battles over for centuries.

CHAPTER SIX

The Spice Islands

Banda Neira was our next destination on the rally after Saumlaki, the fabled Indonesian spice island that contained a mysterious treasure that many European sailors and navigators would risk their lives trying to find for centuries. Some sailors or explorers knew of the island, but did not know how to get there or more importantly, how to get there alive to bring back its much-coveted prize to their queen or king.

Unlike the sailors of the 1500s and 1600s, no crew on our journey were lost due to scurvy, typhoid or the bloody flux, nor did we have to fend off piracy attacks from the pesky

Dutch or Portuguese. It was an easy sail from Saumlaki heading west; the conditions were calm and we comfortably covered the 200 nautical mile journey in two days along with our sailing rally group. The seascape was changing. The ocean depth had plummeted to about 4000 metres, one of the features that made this part of Indonesia so fascinating. Because the colour of the water changed and became an even deeper blue, the sun beams created diamond glimmers as it reflected off the soft waves as we carved our way through. The first sign that we were approaching Banda was the sight of an enormous volcanic mountain covered in dense green jungle that emerged from the sea and reached an astounding 925 metres in height, we were 20 nautical miles from our destination. The mountain island just popped out of the sea as all around there was only water which had a depth of 4000 metres, it was an incredible sight to see the landmarks of a time when the earth's tectonic plates were shifting with so much power and creating volcanoes of such great height.

Next we saw the volcanic island of Pulau Gunung which had a height of 660 metres and formed the outside island of the circular Banda island group that we were sailing to. This volcano had most recently been active in 1988 when it killed hundreds of locals living on the adjacent islands as molten lava and ash cascaded down the outside of the mountainous island and decimated the portside town at Banda Neira. The highly active and fertile soil of the volcanic island had become densely wooded, covered in thick luscious green jungle. The locations where the intensely hot lava flowed into the sea had become a natural phenomenon for active coral and people came to these remote islands from all over the world to dive and snorkel in such beautiful wonder.

The weather, strong seasonal winds – the trade winds which could howl and create choppy seas, were rebuffed by these tall islands that formed a rough circle around a harbour basin and created the anchoring point for us in their centre. A centre which we slowly maneuvered our way to. The only problem was that the water was still very deep at about 80 meters and we could only anchor in about 25 meters, so we inched closer to the shore. The other boats in the rally were ahead of us and had the stern of their boats pointing to the shore as they had reversed in, dropped anchor and stern tied using ropes tied to trees and fences on the shore. The space for anchoring was very tight so to we would be snuggly positioned about two metres from the boat next to us. This was the only option we had, so Hugh followed suit and slowly turned the boat and cautiously reversed closer to the shore. After dropping the anchor and making sure that it grabbed the ocean floor he let the anchor chain extend and complete with some comical gesticulating to some local helpers on shore, we eventually tied the rear of the boat securely to some trees. This meant that we would not swing when the wind or tide changed and bang into the other rally boats tied neatly in a row next to us, or the harbour floor which at that point was very shallow. As I looked below the boat into crystal clear water I could see a dense array of coral and tiny colourful fish.

Aside from the two boats we had befriended – *Kite* and *Hokulea*, we had only spent a few days with the remainder of the group of cruisers we were with when we were all in Darwin and then Saumlaki. Companions in our small sailing group of 12 boats consisted of three American boats who had already sailed one third of the way around the world to get here, one boat from the Netherlands, a couple of boats from New Zealand and a handful of Aussies. We were by far the least experienced and we watched and listened to the more seasoned cruisers for their reactions. A few of our group were experiencing boat problems, one an issue with their engine and another with their steering. The wonderful thing about cruisers is that they pitch in to help if someone has a problem, with tips, advice and spare parts, everyone is quick to try and assist. The cruiser group was a great safety net to have in a place where you would often not find the parts or expertise to fix problems on-shore. Hugh and I listened on the VHF to the chatter of offerings for help and parts as the issues were discussed amongst the group.

Not long after we arrived in Banda, we met Abba. He was a local man, short in stature with a large belly, who had made a business out of catering to tourists, he was the fixer. His offerings included catered accommodation at his family house, walking tours of the island and the sale of obscure relics and artefacts – like old Dutch coins. For the meals, his diminutive and shy wife did the cooking presenting a huge spread of barbequed fish, potato curries and rice dishes. So we, along with our sailing companions on the rally, planned to take Abba up on his offer of a walking tour for the following day.

But that night we enjoyed what had become one of our customary cruiser activities – sundowners, with Jake and Jackie and Jack and Zdenka aboard their boat *Kite*. We all brought some of our food stores like crackers, cheese and the last of our fresh fruit to assemble a nice range of nibblies. Hugh and I also brought some gin, tonic and some limes to celebrate our arrival in such a spectacularly beautiful location. We had all experienced the same mixed sailing conditions and feeling of wonder and anticipation as we entered Indonesia. While our friends had already sailed one third of the world to be here, this was their first entry into Asia and they told us how it was very different to the Pacific Ocean islands that they had visited.

"The dancing and the singing, that is what I remember the most about the Polynesians." said Jackie with a smile, "they gave off such confidence and joy when they danced, they just exuded love and happiness. But with us they were so shy when you spoke to them."

"Yeah, I remember us and a bunch of other boats rolled up to one anchorage in Fiji and after performing for us the locals were sitting on the edge of their seats waiting for us to sing songs or play a guitar, it was just the way that they were used to interacting with each other. Plus, music transcends all language barriers!" said Zdenka as she laughed, "Shame that all the people we were with were so introverted they couldn't get out a note."

"But being here now, there is such a difference in culture to what we have seen. The people are really in your face here, trying to sell something or take a photo of you." said Jake.

"It's quite confronting having people - strangers, so interested in you. It's so different to what I'm used to, I don't like it." said Jackie.

"It's definitely something that we will have to get used to." said Hugh.

The sunset sky turned from a dull orange to a light blue with the darkness falling not long behind. The tall green mountains encircling the small harbour hugged us in. The night wore on and many gin and tonics later, Jake pulled out his favorite bourbon that he had stashed in the bilge of his boat. "This bourbon is for very special occasions only," he said as he rolled the bottle around in his hands looking fondly at the label, "it is my favourite bourbon from back home in Virginia and arriving here in this spectacular location and surviving all of our checking-in requirements for Indonesia is worth celebrating!" he continued as he poured everyone a glass.

"Cheers to that." said Jack.

We clinked our glasses and sipped enjoying the strong flavour of the drink in our mouths. The warmth of spending time with friends combined with arriving at a new port was a moment to treasure and it was a fun night for Hugh and I to get to know the four cruisers better.

The next day our group met Abba at the base of the fort that was built by the Dutch to protect the island group from attack. We were thrust back in time to the 1500s when this island played a critical role in international history. You could see remnants of the Dutch rule in the large black painted canons embossed with the Dutch East India Company logo that lay strewn around the island pointing out to sea.

"So you have now made it to the fabled spice islands. Did you know that hundreds, probably thousands of men from Holland, Portugal and England lost their lives trying to find Banda Neira and bring home its prized spice in the 1600s?" Abba started in his immaculate English. The group of cruisers looked quizzically at Abba as he continued, "And that amazing spice was worth more than gold and was so valued that the land it grew on, the island here that you now stand on in Banda was traded for Manhattan Island by the Dutch?" he said with a grin as he spread his arms wide to indicate the land we were on. The group listened intently, entranced by the story, amazed to be standing on land which was so highly prized and which had faded into the margins of history.

Abba started leading us through the small village where the villagers were all laying out and drying spices. Straight away I could smell the pungent aroma of cloves. The houses that the people lived in were small and made of concrete with corrugated iron roofing. The outside walls of the houses were painted in an array of colours, with one house a vibrant blue, the next a bright pink. The homes had small gardens out the front bounded by low concrete fences which were painted to compliment the house. The streets were packed dirt, which we could see children sweeping with large leafed branches. They stared and giggled when they saw us and some would walk with us for a short way.

Abba led us over to a tree with thin branches which was covered in small green leaves and small brown circular nuts. He picked up a small round nut from the ground. "'Myristica fragrans'," he started, "that's nutmeg by the way. This was that exceptionally valued spice that started a race bringing competent sailors from all over Europe to be the first to find the island and then bring home cargo holds full of the fine soft red centre you will find in that shell - mace. The spice was touted to be the elixir to the flu, to cure the plague and all manner of other afflictions like ageing! Royal heads of state offered lucrative rewards to the explorer that could bring back the nut and even greater rewards were offered for those who could bring it back and cultivate crops outside of this remote location. But in the end it was the Dutch who arrived and held the island. They fought many bloody battles with other Europeans on the hunt and this island was the main reason why the Dutch formed the Dutch East India Company that would dominate world spice and other trading in Asia for over 300 years. You see the Dutch used ownership of the island and therefore the spice to put a stranglehold on supply to Europe and pushed up the value of the spice to exorbitant levels."

The group looked on silently, each fiddling with the small nut as it was passed around and smelling the red mace centre. It had a pungent smell that made my nose crinkle. It seemed incredible that such a small thing, this tiny nut, could be the reason why the entire country of Indonesia was ruled by the Dutch for so many centuries. It was also astounding that this spice could be worth so much and even be the reason why the Dutch and English governments thought it a fair trade when settling their warring debts to trade this island that it grew on for Manhattan, the strategic shipping stronghold of America.

Abba continued his story "and the only reason why Banda stopped being such a prized piece of earth was when an

Englishman under the direction of Sir Stamford Raffles managed to take some Banda island soil to English ruled Singapore and cultivate the nutmeg tree using it. Suddenly the cost for nutmeg plummeted because there was no longer a shortage of supply."

I have never been able to look at the unassuming nutmeg in quite the same way.

CHAPTER SEVEN

Beneath the Surface

I had dropped the anchor and watched the silver coloured chain stretch out over the bow roller as it made its way to the sandy ocean floor 30 meters below. The anchor grabbed and the wind pushed the boat and helped it dig in and secure the boat. We sat back and absorbed the island and the water with our eyes, it was always the first thing that we did when arriving at a new place. The visibility of the water was perfect and I took a moment to breathe in and connect with the wonderous place where we had arrived. The colours of the island were so vibrant, with bright white sand, green grassy shrubs and some enormously tall, bent over, exhausted looking palms with green fronds that looked like they wanted to rest on the sand below. The only signs of human life were the few flimsy huts with palm leaf rooves comprising the rangers' living quarters, a long timber jetty which I suppose was for the supply ship which visited infrequently and an enormously oversized flag – the international red and white symbol for scuba diving - tied to the tallest palm tree flapped invitingly in the breeze, visible for miles.

After five months of sailing we were getting used to the routine activities, the chores, the boring things we had to do to put the boat to rest after sailing. Firstly, we would check the weather to make sure we were safely anchored in case conditions got rough. Next, we would make sure that the anchor was hooked in well, so we put the boat in reverse and checked that the anchor was holding. Sometimes Hugh would swim down and see that it was in a good spot and not tied around a rock or sitting upside down. But that wasn't necessary on this day as the clarity in the water let you see every detail on the ocean floor. Next came the other menial tasks such as packing the boat up – folding the sails and putting the cover over the main to protect it from the relentless beating sun, putting away ropes and other things we don't need while at anchor. Finally, we had a drink and a moment to ponder what to do next. We grabbed the short flier which had a spiel about Take Bone Rate.

"Taka Bone Rate, Indonesia, the third largest atoll in the world and the largest in South-east Asia." read Hugh.

"Huh, I've never heard of it. You?" I asked.

"No, but that must be good right, if no one knows it's here?" he said, "plus, it says here that it is a 16-hour boat ride from the next major city. 16 hours! Only the hardiest of western tourists would tolerate that!"

I chuckled, "yep, no way would I go on a fisherman's boat for the best part of a day, getting dumped on by the daily squalls that pass through in the hope that you arrive alive."

"So here we are in the National Park of the atoll, and there is a resort somewhere over there." he gestured off in the distance through the collection of other small sandy islands. "But this is it for humans, just the rangers on shore and us." looking at our friends on *Kite* and *Hokulea* anchored close by.

Sounded perfect to me. We were so keen for the diving adventures that lay beneath.

While I'd had my license for a while, we had become more and more interested in scuba diving since Hugh had completed his course at one of our first stops in Indonesia. Lucky for us we had buddied up with our amazing cruiser friends who were passionate divers and were also keen to seek out diving spots wherever they could. We knew they would be up for some deep water adventures.

So we got in the VHF radio – this one is for short distance communication to chat with our friends anchored just a hundred meters away.

"Kite, Kite, Kite, this is Elizabeth Jane, over." called Hugh in the customary fashion over the radio.

There was some crackling before "Elizabeth Jane, this is Kite, how're you doin' over there?" asked Jack.

"Yeah, we're all good mate. How are you?" said Hugh.

"Just getting settled in. Trying to dry off after we got dumped on by that rain squall. How beautiful is this place huh?" said Jack.

"I know, we got drenched too. But it is amazing here, worth the soaking sail! We were just reading our book and we can't wait to get a closer look at the reef." said Hugh.

"Oh I know right. We should go ashore and see if we can organise something for tomorrow." said Jack.

"Good plan, do you want to give us a ride in? Oh and we should get Jake along, he'll want to see what's on offer." said Hugh, hoping that we wouldn't have to get our dingy launched and could catch a ride with the others instead.

"Yeah no problem, but you'll have to provide the rum." said Jack.

"Of course, customary taxi fare." said Hugh with a smile.

A trip ashore showed that the view from the boat was close to the reality. There was no mains electricity, a diesel generator got kicked into gear to fill the Rangers empty scuba diving tanks with compressed air once a day. The rangers here did stints of manning the station in a one-month-on, one-month-off rotation. Apart from the abundance of diving they could indulge in, there was not a whole lot to do. It looked like they were just plopped on the island with barely enough food to keep them going for the month. The main table in what looked like their dining room was covered in decks of cards and match sticks which were probably used for gambling with.

We found the ranger that spoke some limited English and he was pleased to take us on a dive tour the next day. He was a man of few words but we managed to communicate that there were five of us diving and he organised a local fisherman to take us to the dive spots in his wooden boat. We could hardly wait!

The next morning, with the typical late arrival that we had begun to expect of the locals, the bright blue and yellow painted wooden boat chugged over to us to pick us up for the day of diving. The fishing boats were all the same, a timber boat with two levels: the level for the driver and his engine way down in the hull and an upper deck area for people to sit or fish from, depending on the purpose of the trip. The engine consisted of a repurposed tractor or truck engine located deep down in the hull attached to a spinning propeller and the driver, standing up, would manoeuvre the throttle and speed by pushing his bare foot on a stick which connected to the engine gears. I marvelled at the skill that they used to do this and the speed that they had when switching between the steering and throttle with their toes. The driver would peer over the upper deck to try and see where he was steering and he could barely see over it he was standing so far below in the hull. The noise was something to behold and rattled your bones. You would never miss a boat coming near you as you could hear it coming from a mile away!

We awkwardly boarded the boat with all our diving gear before the engine roared to life and thundered through the water to the dive site about a 30-minute ride away. I sat on the top deck and enjoyed the ride. On our yacht we travelled at about one tenth the speed and it was a bit of a thrill to move so fast on the fisherman's boat and have the salty air rush at my face. Once arriving at the dive site, we got ready. I always struggled getting into the wetsuit and the rest of the diving gear, but Hugh helped me and we did our usual buddy checks to make sure we were set. We counted 'One-Two-Three' and rolled backwards off the boat to fall into the refreshing water below. When we did that it would always prompt me to take a big suck in on my air supply as a rush of cold water penetrated through my wetsuit. Once again the water was amazingly clear and we could see the sunlight refracting golden patterns off the ripples in the water surface and the swaying coral in the shallows below. We moved off to where the guide was gesturing us to follow. From here on it would be hand signals for communication while we tried to capture it all with our eyes. Around us we could see bright soft corals waving in the current and hard corals forming the solid part of the reef floor. The range of different types of coral seemed limitless. It was as if we were swimming in an underwater rainforest adorned with vibrant oranges, pinks, blues, greens and yellows, so bright they could probably glow in the dark.

We reached the edge of the reef and started to descend the side of the reef wall. The further we descended the more the water colour went from light to deep impenetrable blue below. The water depth dropped off significantly to about 1000 metres and I began to feel this sense of unease that I could not see the bottom, or see what was below as the deepening colour swallowed and hid life. It was a strange fear to have as we sailed over water that was much deeper than this, but I suppose fears are rarely rational. The water temperature dropped incrementally the further from the surface we descended. I kept myself focused on looking at the amazing array of sea life flittering around the coral wall. Tiny clown fish with bright orange and white striped bodies ducked and weaved in and out of the sea anemones that they call home. The clown fish opened and closed their mouths, silently mouthing at me to "go away!" and used the soft flapping edges of the anemone tentacles for cover to protect their domain. Further along the wall there were nudibranchs, tiny brightly coloured creatures which can vary so much in their shape and colours you wonder how they could all belong to one species.

I checked my air gauge, not long to go now. I tuned into my breathing to make sure I was taking slow breaths and timing my use of the tank's air to conserve it. Then barely ten metres away we noticed a large and magnificent green hawksbill turtle crunching on some coral before spotting us - its predator, and it started to awkwardly move off the coral and swim with the current. It started off by waving its right fin and then its left which made its way from side to side in an uneven fashion as it developed the momentum to use both fins together and swim coordinated and confidently away from us. I was so absorbed in watching the turtle that I didn't realise our time was up. Hugh grabbed my arm and gestured that he was heading to the surface and I should join him.

We emerged at the surface and immediately pulled our masks off. "How amazing was that dive!" Hugh said.
"Totally cool." said Jake. "I could spend forever watching those tiny little anemones, they were so vibrant."
"I know right, and how about that turtle, I almost missed it because I was staring at those micro fish rushing around the coral trying to hide from us." said Jack.
"I loved watching that turtle, they move so ungracefully when they are getting up momentum!" I said, grinning.

We each clambered aboard the fishing boat removing our heavy diving gear first and passing it up, I felt as ungainly as the turtle swimming away trying to hoist myself back on the boat.

After we arrived back to the ranger's island from our diving we went for a walk along the eastern beach. This time of year it was the windward side which meant that the wind blew very strong and the surf was powerful. As we walked along the sand we were shocked to see the sand covered in waste, plastic bottles, plastic bags and old thongs that had washed up on the shore with the tides and the wind. This island generated very little waste and the rangers did not bring much with them when they came on their shifts. There was even a motorbike bumper tangled in some of the beach grass. I walked behind the others and could see Hugh's shoulders drop as he saw the amount of rubbish piling up with each incoming wave. He sighed as he started kicking through a collection of rubber thongs and even a kid's bicycle. "I can't believe how much stuff there is and it's all floating in from the other neighbouring islands. This is what is going to kill this place."
"We've seen it everywhere we've been, Hugh," said Jake. "We just went on this amazing dive, but this is the reality. The rubbish will choke the reef and the sea life that live here." said Hugh in flat weary voice.
"That's the contradiction of Indonesia, Hugh," said Jake "it has these beautiful lands and waters that are being put

under massive pressure from surrounding development. Protecting the environment is barely something that is understood by the government so where would the leadership come from?" he asked.

I looked solemnly out to sea, there was so much education and infrastructure that needed to come ahead of any serious change to pollution issues like this one, I really hoped that we could come back again in 20 years and see the place in a better condition rather than a worse one. I picked up a clump of old tangled fishing net and carried it with me back to our dingy to dispose of in our rubbish bag, it was a futile attempt to save one dolphin or turtles life.

CHAPTER EIGHT

The Rainforest Island

It was the mannerisms of the orangutans that really struck me first. They are so closely related to us humans and I could tell that by looking at their eyes. They felt emotions and wanted to protect their young. The problem was that their world was being destroyed piece by piece by human development and they were becoming slaves to their handlers, to the organisations that provided a jungle sanctuary for them and provided them food. Most of the orangutans no longer hunted in the jungle for their food, but squabbled over the food given to them with the other apes, while we took photos of them and watched our distant cousins in what was a fight for survival.

We were nearing the end of our Indonesian adventure and had decided to go on a river boat trip, joining our friends Jack and Zdenka and Jacks' brother and sister-in-law who had flown in to Kalimantan, Borneo for a visit. We had left our yachts and gone on a three-day tour with a local company in their small timber river boat called a *klotok* as our sailing boats were too big to travel down the water inlets. Most of the other cruisers from our group were also on the river, however they travelled in separate klotoks.

As with the other Indonesian boats we had been on, the driver was deep down in the belly of the boat kicking over a diesel truck engine that would roar to life and shake the boat with a loud putt-putt-putt as it was slowly steered through the winding river bends. The timber was painted a bright glossy green with yellow trimming. There were two levels, the lowest for the engine; where the driver and the guide sat while we were underway, and the upper deck for us to sit and view the jungle as we slowly moved by. There was a low lying timber roof above us to protect us from the harsh sun or rain. The river was hemmed in by brilliant green low-lying river shrubbery including napal palms that overhung the water and made it seem narrower than it was. The murky-brown river twisted and turned and the sky above was an ominous dark grey. Less than an hour into our trip rain began teaming down accompanied by lightning and thunder. We huddled on our houseboat as our guide pulled down tarpaulin walls to protect the inside of the boat from becoming saturated.

It was a few hours until we were at the entry to the National Park and the rain had eased for our first visit into the rainforest park. We walked off the boat along a short timber boardwalk and into a clearing where there were two or three small timber and corrugated iron huts. From one of these huts emerged a Park Ranger - Taman. He was an Indonesian man and small in stature with dark chocolate brown skin. He wore an immaculately ironed khaki green shirt with the national park emblem on his left breast pocket and matching green knee length shorts. In broken English he started to tell us about the lifecycle and challenges for the orangutans.

"Many of orangutans in park were rescued orphans. Logging for palm oil plantations and mining activities have risk tha orangutan habitat and now threatened to extinction. Parks provide place where life cycle continue and new generation of wil' orangutans can grow. We hope new generation will survive in wil' without relying on us nomore." Taman started. The group were crowded and hushed while Taman was talking. "It hard for tha orangutan because tha mating cycle is verr long. Tha female is pregnant nine month and after carry baby on back or chest for eight or nine years. No mating until baby leaves. A female might have four babies in her lifetime, it is har' for re-population. Also tha orangutans here don't go back to wil' because they have contact with human, they never go back, they rely on us giving food." Taman started walking and leading us down a dirt path into a dense jungle area.

The light became dimmer as the trees above us crowded in and provided a dense green roof, filtering the sun and making it feel later in the day than it was. There were some gaps in the tree coverage where shards of light would shoot to the jungle floor as we clambered over mud, fallen trees and soft leafy carpets. The tall trees around us were covered in a green and brown moss that was slowly enveloping all their limbs. Due to the humidity, the moisture in the air settled on trees and the jungle floor and I was amazed at how wet everything was, just touching the tree trunks left you with a wet hand. The sound of our feet on the ground was muffled by the dirt path that was slightly muddy. We neared the end of the path and we could hear the animals before we saw them, calling through the jungle to each other and hanging on to the topmost bendy branches of trees to swing with a loud crashing sound onto the next tree. They avoided walking along the jungle floor, they felt safer up high, able to watch and inspect us from above.

There was only one orangutan that made its way to the feeding station which comprised a small raised wooden deck. The rangers had left a large hessian bag of sweet potato, banana and open coconuts. We stood at a distance so as not to appear a threat to the orangutans.

"Careful, as orangutan verr strong, can hurt verr bad if you scare or she worry about baby." said Taman.

We saw one female orangutan tentatively climb down a tree to the deck landing with a thud, she had a baby clinging to her chest hair. What struck me about the orangutan was the similarities in their appearance to humans. They are such a close relative on the evolutionary scale and have many mannerisms and physical features that we have. She had deep brown or black skin covered in a thick orange coat of hair that licked the sides of her face, feet and hands, she moved around on her two back legs rarely using her forearms to move. Her dark brown eyes looked quickly around from left to right to make sure that she and her baby were safe. Satisfied, the mother deftly peeled the skin of the bananas and made her way through handful after handful of the food while still hanging with one arm on a woody vine, always watching and ready to scale the tree if threatened. Her baby looked around with glistening eyes, not one to miss an eating opportunity, helped himself to his mother's milk. Mesmerised, the group stood gaping at the animal as she fed and checked her baby was doing fine as she hurriedly made her way through the bag of food.

Eventually the orangutan had finished eating and made her way back to the high canopy. We returned down the jungle path to the klotok for some afternoon tea of banana fritters. As the afternoon rolled into evening, we were gifted with a most spectacular sunset, lighting the belly of the clouds with a pink hue. Our guide expertly picked a tranquil river location to stop the boat for the sunset on the klotok, lit by fireflies. The scene was amazing, with hundreds of little flitters of golden light dancing around a small bush as darkness descended. The fireflies made short zapping sounds as they zipped around each other providing our evening entertainment while our guides cooked us dinner in the lower section of the boat.

We relaxed after our dinner of grilled river fish to listen to the sound of the marshy forest as the nocturnal insects and animals came to life. We started talking about the orangutans.
"They are much bigger than I imagined." I said.
"I know right. But they seem so meek when you think about their struggle. An animal that impressive could be wiped out because we want to use their jungle land for other things." said Zdenka.
"We've all heard about their habitat diminishing, but to see the impact really is devastating." said Jack.
"You go to the shops and they sell palm oil for cooking in four or five litre bottles and it is subsidised! I mean cooking

oil is cheap anyway, but to make it cheaper is just shocking. It is just hopeless for the orangutan." said Hugh. "The oil isn't just for cooking with either, it's in everything, like bread, soap, cosmetics. We're ruining the world." I said.

"Travelling around on a boat feels like you really get exposed to what we are doing to the environment. The mining, rubbish, pollution, over fishing, you can see it all when you live on a boat." said Zdenka.

Hugh looked down into his wine glass and I looked off the side of the boat into the jungle. A jungle that seemed to be diminishing by the minute, strangling the future of the orangutan.

We never concluded the conversation and sat in silence for a while before deciding to go to sleep for the night. We each slept on single mattresses on the floor that our guide had brought up from the lower level of the boat, with a mosquito net hanging from the ceiling over us. As I drifted off to sleep I could hear the mosquitos buzzing and soft rustling of nocturnal animals in the foliage of the jungle next to our boat.

The following morning we awoke at five o'clock to the sounds of a hooting gibbon heralding the day as the first glimmers of light streaked across the sky. Our driver kicked the engine into gear as we ventured further still in the jungle. After two hours we turned down a different fork in the river and the water clarity cleared up. Our guide told us that the brown silty dirt in the river was from silica mining which pollutes the entire river for kilometres. We could see that while we were in a national park, there was logging and mining all around, testing the ability of the government to protect the land. The river bank vegetation had changed and now high trees lined the banks. The river opening became so narrow our klotok was pushing branches aside to forge through. We were going to another sanctuary in the jungle and observed a different group of orangutans being fed some fruit and vegetables which happened twice daily. These sanctuaries seemed to be providing the last opportunity to keep the Orangutan population alive and in their natural habitat. It was good to visit them to enable their continued work in the hope that the orangutan habitat could be saved before it was too late and totally destroyed here in Borneo.

The three days on the boat tour were coming to an end and our driver meticulously maneuvered the boat in the narrow river and turned the boat around and slowly motored back through the riverways and emerged in the Kumai River not far from the town where the journey had begun. As we returned to the industrial harbour of Kumai town, it was visually a stark contrast to the brilliant green of the National Park. The west side of the river shore was dominated by the concrete and dust of a grimy town and the east side by the bold green jungle that licked at the waters edge. A grey haze settled late in the day and hung low into the night, it was the smoke from the forest fires - the method used to clear land for development, palm plantations, mining or rice farming.

The following morning we sailed from Kumai. A dense haze sat over the river and the channel was busy with commercial shipping; transporting lumber, mined silica, gold and wood chips. Using the ebbing tide, we were pushed out of the Kumai river and its brown silty water to the clear blue of the Java Sea.

CHAPTER NINE

Lightning

It was only ten o'clock but the morning sky had turned a dark shade of grey and the humidity was so high that I could feel the sweat beading before it trickled down the side of my face. I had learnt over the seven months or so we had spent in Indonesia and Malaysia that this was a sign that the weather was about to change - and change fast. The boat was anchored in the narrow Johor Strait, the water separating Malaysia and Singapore in lightning alley - an area very close to the equator and known for its unpredictable storms. It's called the inter-tropical convergence zone – the ITCZ – where the north-east and south-west trade winds come together; a meeting place of differing weather systems that creates still, dull stagnant calms accompanied by very high humidity peppered with violent and often intense storms or squalls. The high humidity creates the elements required for thunderstorms and this location sees thousands of severe thunderstorms a year, but this one created an ominous feeling in the pit of my stomach. I started to feel nervous about what the morning could bring.

Hugh had just dingied towards the Malaysian town of Johor Bahru to run some errands. I was in charge of the boat, a day of leisure while at anchor ahead of our departure a few days later. I pottered about, making tea and doing some chores then reading a book. I could hear the thunder rumbling in the distance, though the sun was still blazing down from above. I thought the storm would just roll off to disappear in another direction. But I still couldn't settle; something didn't feel right. I pre-emptively made my way through the boat, closing all the hatches, pulling in items off the deck, and generally made ready for a downpour. Once satisfied I nestled into my favourite seat in the cabin and returned to my book.

Suddenly a loud BOOM jolted me, and in my haste to run up to the deck I accidentally knocked over my cup of water on the cabin floor. I scrambled around to mop up my mess and emerged from the cabin to see the ugliest, fiercest looking cloud and wall of rain steadily making its way towards me. I could see the rain on the water as it pummeled the surface. It was so heavy I could not see through it to the land on the other side. The earlier anxiety crested into fear as a feeling of dread overcame me. I had no idea what was coming and what I could do about it. I checked the hatches and portholes were closed-up and impatiently waited, sitting down in the cockpit and tapping my hands on my knees.

A lightning strike to your boat is an event that would make many a sailor go pale just thinking about. It can disable the electrical systems, including the navigation instruments, radar, radios, lights, onboard devices like phones, computers and laptops. Even worse, it can shoot through the boat and out the other side leaving a catastrophic hole in the hull. In *Moby Dick,* the story set on a timber whaling ship which was inconveniently full of flammable whale oil, a lightning strike hits the boat and like a match to a petrol can, sets off a blaze in the mast and engulfs the whole boat. While a fictional story, it encourages the most fanciful visions in the imagination. Risk of fire aside, we'd heard from a boat surveyor that had to x-ray the rigging of boats for internal structural damage to the stainless-steel fixtures after lighting strikes. We had also met some other cruisers who were grounded in Malaysia for a year after a lightning bolt ran up their anchor chain and fried their electrical systems.

The wind came before the rain and I could feel the boat dancing on the anchor. The wind blast was strong and I was intrigued at its speed, so I hopped up and turned the instruments on to see a reading of 30 knots. If we were sailing it would be advance notice that we should furl some sails in and prepare for heavy weather. I started pacing in small steps back and forth. I began to shiver as the wind was cold on my skin and such a contrast to the heat of the early morning. Another blast of cold wind brought the rain. I looked out and saw the black sky and rain pounding the deck and creating a wall of white reducing my visibility. I sat in the cockpit and shivered as a bright white lightning bolt stung the water like an angry snake barely 400 metres from the back of the boat and the heavens released an almighty BOOM of thunder. I clapped my hands over my ears and fell to my knees on the cockpit floor, buckled by the intense sound of the thunder. By then, I was shaking with fear, my knuckles white, my mind racing. I felt completely alone.

Suddenly Hugh's words came back to me.
"If you are ever in a lightning storm, put everything in the faraday cage." he said.
"What's a faraday cage?" I asked.
Hugh opened his electrical text book and read aloud in his lecturer tone "ahem… 'a faraday cage is a steel box which provides a shield from static electric currents by distributing it around the cage instead of through electronic

devices. The electrical current of the strike would destroy the inner working of unprotected electrical devices'. Using the oven to achieve this is an age-old trick touted by cruisers as a great way to try and protect onboard items."

"So you put our phones, laptops, GPS and stuff in the oven?" I asked.

"Yes."

"It sounds ridiculous."

"It's all about the metal, it will protect our backup nav equipment. Trust the science."

Typical Hugh to always be so logical when it comes to justifying something.

"But it is very important to remember to take them out again before using the oven for cooking." he said.

"Obviously." I laughed with an eye roll.

Gingerly I pulled myself up, took two steps before swinging into action and quickly turned all the instruments off and all of the other circuits on the switch panel. I moved around the cabin of the boat grabbing our internet dongle, laptops and handheld GPS thinking about what else I should put in the oven. I remembered the cameras and memory drives and they went in too. I was racking my brain trying to think of anything else I needed to do. I was sure there was something I was forgetting but my heart was pumping so fast and was so loud in my head I couldn't think straight. Another lightning bolt struck the water even closer to the boat and an enormous CRACK erupted upon impact, followed immediately by a boneshaking BOOM of thunder. I could feel my resolve slipping. My body was shaking. The storm was coming closer and I was powerless to stop it.

The wind picked up again and I could hear the screaming of the rigging. The boat was heeling from the pressure of the wind, throwing the boat powerfully over to its port side. The angle and speed of the wind at 45 knots was creating the 'singing' of the rigging as the wind whipped through it. Crouching in the cockpit I remembered from some books I had read of ancient fables where sailors talked about the 'singing' of the rigging in the wind, like that of a finely tuned violin. I had not heard it on our boat before and thought that maybe ours did not sing. It turns out that it just needed the right provocation. All around it sounded like a quartet of violins tuning before a performance and the rushing sound of wind trying to push through the bimini fabric that protected our cockpit. The boat came upright again as the wind eased off, but suddenly heeled again as another gust blasted through. I thought for sure things would start flying off the boat. We had lashed the items on the deck down with rope which managed to keep them in place and thankfully they stayed put.

Just as the wind began to ease off, another lightning bolt hit the water with a CRACK and again the atmosphere vibrated with the BOOM of thunder. The storm was directly above me now as I hunkered down, shivering in the cockpit, with hands about my ears like a small child. It was the most chilling feeling I can remember; I was terrified. The feeling of helplessness threatened to overwhelm me as I could only watch as the lightning smacked the water time and again like a live wire dancing in front of my eyes. The minutes ticked by and after what seemed like an age, although was probably only fifteen minutes or whatever, the storm started to dissipate. The rain moved off in a northerly direction. It was finally over, I had survived and so had the boat.

It took a while for my heart to slow down and return to normal. This was my first real test on the boat on my own. Thankfully we did not get struck by lightning and I had remembered the important things like packing away our navigation equipment in case we did get struck. I sat down and took some long slow breaths. The feelings inside were at odds with the outside world as sunlight streamed through the clouds and beamed down. The humid heat of the day returned as the water quickly dried on the deck.

A few hours later Hugh arrived back at the boat and I relayed the story of the storm and the things I did. "I'm so sorry you were alone for that. As I sped off in the dingy I quickly looked behind me and I could see the looming black clouds, I didn't realise that it would be so intense and so close to the boat. I'm so glad that you're okay." said

Hugh as he hugged me, "as I was coming back here in the dingy over the choppy waves I could tell that this area got whipped up by the wind."

"Yeah, well I'm glad that you were able to keep ahead of it. Being in the dingy you would have practically got sunk by the amount of rain that fell!" I said.

"I managed to stay ahead of it and get to the shops before the storm hit. But I had to spend about 10 minutes pumping all the rainwater out of the dingy when I got back to it." he said, "but I'm so impressed by the actions you took; turning off the switches and putting the electronics in the oven. I can't believe you remembered to do all that. You would have definitely reduced the damage to the boat if there was any stray lightning strike near the boat."

"All those conversations we had while at sea, the 'what if' scenarios. All well-rehearsed by us in theory."

"And all those conversations with cruisers at the bar, everyone has a lightning story and what they did to get through it. Well, whatever happened, I'm so glad that you're okay. It's a bonus that the boat is fine too, we have you to thank for that." Hugh said as he squeezed my shoulder.

At that point, I couldn't wait to get out of this area, but little could I imagine that it would be almost another year until we would be out of the ITCZ.

CHAPTER TEN

A Perfect Christmas

The hundreds of timber fishing boats lighting up the horizon and filling our ears with their loud drumming engines dominated the 14 hour overnight sail from the Thai tourist town of Khao Lak. The 70 nautical mile journey meant that it was just a bit too far for us to complete in one daytime. The blinding lights of the fishing boats created glowing domes on the horizon, contrasting with the inky black night as the moon was rising late. This darkness made it possible to see the vivid phosphorescents flicker to life as we disturbed the water on our way north. On deck on my own, I looked up to catch the wind on my cheek and spotted shooting stars tracking across the dark canvas overhead. It was a glorious warm night for sailing, the light easterly wind filling our sails in a comfortable beam reach making for light work aboard and plenty of time to soak up the beauty that the ocean had to offer. The blinding lights of the squid fishing boats burned my retinas and ruined the night vision I was trying to develop, thankfully the further we pushed away from the mainland the less squid boats we passed and the more alone we felt. The last four weeks we had spent in Thailand we had felt anything but alone. The tourist trade there was a big deal and anything worth seeing was totally swamped with local tourism operators and all the noise that they bring. Being on a yacht really spoilt you for seeking out remote and quiet places. Since we had started on our voyage, we had developed quite an aversion to busy tourist spots.

The night was marked by our usual rotating three-hour helming shifts. These started at 6pm after dinner when I went down below to catch some rest while Hugh manned things up on deck. We had an agreement that we would wake the other if help was needed managing the sails or if there was a storm coming. At 9pm we swapped and Hugh went to get some shut-eye while I captained the boat, this rotation went on until around 6am when the sun rose and we would share the tasks of steering the boat throughout the day and have naps to catch up on any missed sleep. When the weather was rough it was the hardest time to rest as it could be very difficult to sleep with the motion of the boat and the noise that the waves made crashing into the boat hull could wake the dead. Those were the hard nights. But this night was different, it was comparatively serene and a perfect sailing leg.

Four weeks earlier we had started planning for where we would be at Christmas, but the problem with sailing is that you have to take all plans with the assumption that they will probably change. Something always gets in the way: it might be adverse weather or something breaks on the boat to delay any sailing. And just two weeks earlier we broke our anchor windlass - the winch machine that hauled up our anchor and all its 80 kilograms of weight from the ocean floor. After it broke, Hugh got tired of pulling the anchor up, link-by-link each day and we diverted our route so that we could go to Phuket to have an engineer re-fashion the bushings in the electric winch motor. Around this time our batteries also failed, which meant that we only had some measly electricity from the solar panels which left us with no power overnight. So we scaled back our use of laptop chargers, radio, the water pump and lights and we decided to delay solving that problem for a few weeks when we would be able to get new batteries delivered while docked in a marina. Even with these setbacks we hoped to make it to the Surin Islands for Christmas, it was only a few days sail from Phuket heading north and just on the border of Thailand and Myanmar.

To make it to our Christmas destination, we spent about a week slowly making our way up the western side of the Thai peninsula. Three days prior to our final overnight sail to the Surin Islands from the mainland we had our last task to complete, to pick up supplies from the local town markets in Khao Lak for our on-board Christmas feast. This was going to be a real splurge from our usual boat fare which was heavy on the vegetarian options.

"Do you think they have any meat here?" I asked, as we weaved our way through the fresh food market stalls.

"They must! Just follow your nose!" said Hugh as he picked up a potato and pointed to a pumpkin on one stall. We continued making our way through the market, looking in different rows to see what was on offer. Then he started gesturing to me from a few rows over "it's here, they've got everything!"

As I made my way over to where Hugh was standing I could see flies hovering over the fresh meat that was laid out on tables. This was the pretty typical market shopping we had come to expect. We had to try our luck that the meat had not been out too long and didn't harbour any nasties, we tried to get to these markets early in the morning to improve our chances. I could see Hugh looking through the different cuts of what looked like pork, then he found the one he was after, a huge piece with the fatty skin still on. Of course he wanted to do crackling with his roast meat!

"What part of the pig is this from?" Hugh started to ask the stall owner, but she didn't speak English, so he switched tack. He pointed to his shoulder and she looked confused. Then he pointed to his leg and she shook her head. Finally he pointed to his bottom and the lady giggled and nodded. "Looks like we got some pork rump" he said to me with a big grin on his face. With our bags of fresh food and after buying our customary iced coffee which we always bought while on-shore, we were back in the motorbike taxi and off to the boat.

With dawn spreading a pink hue across the grey sky on this the morning before Christmas Day, I steered us around the southern end of the Surin Island chain, focused on the task of making sure that we made a safe entry as the wind whipped up to 25 knots. The timing of our arrival was perfect with the sun of the new day to guide us through some rocky outcrops. We turned into a sheltered bay and I was amazed by the clear water and aqua coloured reef at the base of jungle-covered hummocks. Moored alone in this beautiful bay we knew that we had picked the perfect spot for our first sailing Christmas away.

After a quick morning sleep and some breakfast we headed out. Snorkeling around the coral-filled bay was the best way to shake off an overnight sail. We spotted clown fish, sweet lips, moray eels, clams, and I listened to the crunching sounds of the parrot fish munching on the coral heads. Above the water, a refreshing wind kept the 38-degree heat of the day pleasant, providing us with a clear blue sky as a backdrop to the green jungle tumbling down the hills. The glittering diamonds of sunshine on the water made the spot all the more idyllic. The day disappeared as we relaxed on deck and overcame the wave of exhaustion that always struck us after overnight passages. This time was especially bad and it reminded us that we were out of shape from doing overnight sailing legs. The past two months we had been doing easy short day sails from port to port throughout Malaysia and Thailand and overnight passages took some conditioning to get accustomed to.

Later that day we busied ourselves with more snorkeling and some exploration of the dense jungle ashore. After some time on shore we returned to the boat to do some interior Christmas decorating. A pineapple draped with solar powered fairy lights was our makeshift Christmas tree with a small yellow rubber ducky as the angel. Family and friends had been kind enough to give us some Christmas presents almost eight months earlier when we left Sydney so I placed them under the 'tree' ready for the following day. We sat up on deck to watch the bright red orb of a sun set over the ocean and toasted our blessings with rum cocktails.

Christmas day was another hot tropical day. We woke to a normal breakfast of toast from my homemade bread then started unwrapping the presents. In the collection we had some second hand books and DVDs which Krissy had lovingly wrapped and had been sitting in our boat hide-holes waiting for their big day. Perfect for us as we had just about consumed every book and movie on the small collection we brought with us.

Next - to prepare for the lunch feast I got busy peeling carrots and potatoes, cutting pumpkin and beans. Hugh's eyes lit up when I pulled the piece of pork from the fridge. He had been waiting a very long time for some pork after the five months we had spent in Muslim countries that did not sell or serve pork. We set the oven and moved up on deck to relax reading new books and absorbing the scenery and the silence. The oven was a moody beast and it took hours to cook our dinner so we got busy enjoying delicious rum drinks. It was beginning to feel like we had accomplished something having been away for eight months and sailed through five countries. I mean we had really developed our sailing skills, weathered some storms and were just getting into the groove of this whole cruiser lifestyle. We were also definitely stronger together than when we had started off and we had developed an understanding of each other's needs and how to get by in a confined space.

It was mid afternoon in the heat of the day when we tucked into our feast of a dinner. It was a strange feeling to be enjoying a traditional English-style Christmas roast in the tropical waters of Thailand, but hey, sometimes you just need a bit of home on special occasions. Hugh couldn't stop smacking his mouth while he tucked into the pork. It seemed this was exactly what he needed to round out the adventure so far - to what would be the most western point of our journey. We had decided a few weeks ago that this was going to be our turning around point and from here we would sail back east to get home to Sydney. Eastward sailing is known as 'the wrong way round' because it is against the trade winds and sailors often encounter inhospitable weather, so it was a big decision to make. We had realised though that if we were not intending to sail further west to South Africa, then this was the logical point to stop and return home – going east.

Sharing a sense of achievement of the journey to date, we spent the rest of the afternoon with full bellies and a deep satisfaction in how far we'd come together. We didn't know that the most challenging sailing trips were yet to come and our happy feelings of the day would melt away as we questioned our decisions to sail east out of Thailand on the tough journey home.

CHAPTER ELEVEN

Encounter with a Rat

It was months after our magical Christmas dinner, and we were holed up in a Malaysian marina waiting for the seasons to turn. There was a lull in our journey as we waited for the prevailing monsoon wind to turn from north-easterly to the south-westerly for us to sail to the other side of the Malaysian peninsular. The weather was stiflingly stagnant and hot. We had done maintenance jobs on the boat, visited the local food hawker markets and taken our day-trips to Singapore in search of boat parts. But we wanted a break, a chance to see other parts of Asia that we could not sail to. So we decided to go on a short two-week holiday to Vietnam via plane and had returned to our boat.

After the holiday we were exhausted from our travel back to the boat compounded by a bout of food poisoning that I picked up from eating some local Indian food in Kuala Lumpur. Even though it was only ten o'clock in the morning when we returned, I had been dreaming of lying down on our bed with a pillow cushioning my weary head as my aching bones sunk into the mattress, listening to the water softly lapping the side of the hull. But that thought vanished when we arrived back to the boat to find evidence of a visitor: a jagged round hole in the timber companionway door about the size of an orange and timber shavings on the cockpit cushions. Unease came over me as we slowly explored what had happened in our absence. We cautiously moved cushions and looked for other markers to tell more of the story, but there were none to be found. Hugh fumbled around and pulled the keys out of his pocket, slowly unlocking the padlocked companionway door. Then he stepped inside the boat and disappeared from view of the cockpit.

"Oh, no." said Hugh.
I peeked my head into the open companionway to try and see what he was exclaiming at.
"Ohhhh, noooooo." he repeated with more exasperation.
I stepped down the ladder into the boat to see what he'd found. "What the hell happened here?" I asked, turning up my nose at the smell of curdled milk.

"Oh god I don't know. But I think it's safe to say that we didn't have any human intruders, more the rat variety."

"Ewwww." I swallowed, feeling sick at the thought. I looked around the boat to see evidence of rat poo and things slightly displaced. Hugh was shuffling some papers on the nav desk and I went over to check in the electrical box which was right next to it.

"No, no, don't worry about in there, I will check it and see what happened." he mumbled and shooed me away in an unusually hurried fashion. "Why don't you go check other parts of the cabin?"

I was put off by his sudden insistence that I leave it alone, but got distracted by the thought of other things the rat could have destroyed and started moving through the boat. We couldn't actually see the rat, so we hoped that it had left the boat.

For the next hour Hugh got busy reading about rats on the internet. "Can you believe this? It says here that 'a single rat may ruin 10 times as much food as it eats. And what they don't eat they chew: wood, PVC, plastic, paper and electric cable are but a few of the things rats like to use to sharpen their teeth. Boats provide a perfect rat home being dry, warm and generally having food to eat'. I feel like we are in some kind of rat paradise here. We have to go and get some rat killing tools!" he said with some excitement as he hopped up from his seat. Anything for a trip to the hardware store.

For the remainder of the trip we were always cautious about rats and other vermin coming on the boat. We went on to nickname the rat 'Russell' and I would twitch and snap my head around if I ever thought I heard scratching sounds coming from a drawer. For months afterwards, he haunted me. Rats are so damn destructive the way that they can eat through electrical cables, food stores and parts of the boat. We were in a part of the world that is notorious for rats boarding boats and we still had no idea how he got in as we were quite diligent about closing entry points. It seemed from the companionway door hole that he had nibbled his way out, perhaps to go and stretch his legs one day after eating all that he desired in the boat. The little critter had eaten most of the food supplies that we had been storing for the long months ahead exploring the remote outlying islands of Borneo and northern Indonesia. So over the next few days we spent many trips restocking our stores like rice, flour, UHT milk, tea, coffee and sugar. But we were lucky as he didn't eat any of the crucial boat systems so no major boat repairs were required.

Three days later I was moving some things around in the aft cabin. Opening some drawers and looking for some clean pillow covers.
"Oh my god, he's here, he's HERE, HE'S STILL HERE!" I wailed.
Hugh rushed over from the other side of the cabin "what, I don't see anything."

"Just listen."

We stood silently as we heard a scratching sound coming from the drawer under our bed.

Hugh grabbed the fishing spear and held it menacingly above the closed drawer, ready to pounce.

"What do you think you are going to do with that? That's ridiculous. Put it away before you punch a hole in the bottom of our boat!" I laughed and grabbed it off him.

Hugh slowly pulled open the drawer and I backed away, leaving him to be the fodder of the rat that I had built up in my head as the size of a cat with red eyes and frothy jowls. We had been sharing a boat with him for three days now, unable to catch him in the sophisticated rat trap system we had set up throughout the boat. But the little weasel had created a nifty tunnel system by nibbling through the drawer wall and quickly skittered off through his network of hideholes to another out-of-reach spot under the bed before Hugh could do any catching or trapping.

After that experience we knew we had to fetch some more rat catching supplies. And much to the enjoyment of the hardware store worker at Johor, Hugh told the story of Russell and showed the photo of the companionway door with the large hole. The worker gave us his 'mouse traps' that were fit for a cat and we headed back to the boat. With a maniacal fervor Hugh got busy practicing the traps on pencils, laughing with glee as the pencil would snap in two and spin across the boat. We were fairly confident that the traps would be up to the task. But the rat was sharper than that and outsmarted us time and time again.

More days passed of missed rat-catching opportunities and I became increasingly enraged by this tiny animal that was wreaking havoc on our small boat home. I would storm about the boat swearing and flinging open doors to try and spot the monster, with no hope of trapping or removing it. It was really a futile outpouring of emotion. While Hugh could see me getting more and more upset, he, too, was worried that the critter might eat some important electrical wires. So he decided it was time to get serious and made a second trip to the hardware store and brought home a live trap. This metal cage was a bit bigger than a shoe box and had metal bars all the way around it and a door that snapped shut when the animal was inside the cage. We liked the metal as we were confident that Russell would not be able to chew his way out once captive. That night we placed the cage at the entry to the galley and decorated the inside with some stinky canned cat food.

The next morning at 6 a.m. I walked into the galley and rubbed my eyes from another fitful night sleep filled with rat visions and saw a big brown Russell looking very unimpressed in the live rat trap. I let out the biggest most obtuse cackle.

Hugh quickly came out to the galley from the cabin after he heard my cackle and was shocked to see the look of rage and glee in my eyes. "I don't know who you are. This rat has evoked some kind of demonic witch."

"Haha! This monster has been stealing my sleep, eating our food and stinking up our house, his time has come! You can't tell me you are enjoying his company can you?"

Hugh looked at the rat and shrugged his shoulder with a sarcastic smirk.

I shook my head at him, "But I don't think that I can kill him, you'll have to do that part."

"Oh really. What do you think I am supposed to do with him?"

"I don't know, send him swimming?" I suggested.

We continued to set the trap for weeks afterwards, just to make sure. I would wake up dreaming of rats and go fossicking through the drawers looking for signs of Russell or his babies. Despite cleaning every corner of the boat to remove his smell and mess, I couldn't erase the memories. That was one traumatic experience and one that I didn't want to relive.

So from then on, we routinely closed the hatches and attached metal chew-proof wire sheets to the companionway door to ensure there were no uninvited visitors.

CHAPTER TWELVE

Friends and Goodbyes

Saying goodbye, it was always the hardest part of sailing, but something that we had to get used to as it was part and parcel of the cruiser life. Goodbye was a bit too definite and in sailing you never know what is going to happen, so we started to say 'see you later'. On the dock next to their boat we embraced our friends Jack and Zdenka. "Now you Ozzies make it home safe okay?" said Jack in his crisp New Yorker accent.

We were almost a year into our sailing adventure, a year since we had pushed off the dock in Sydney. It was another hot and humid day in mainland Malaysia, our time there was finally drawing to a close as the seasonal change was upon us which brought favourable winds for us to travel east to Borneo. It had been a long six months in Malaysia and we were looking forward to seeing the other island of the country – Borneo. Waiting for the wind had been tedious and we were itching to get going again. At our marina in Johor Bahru we had been consumed doing chores on the boat, recovering from the rat incident, replacing parts or doing boat maintenance to make sure she was in top shape for more sailing.

"Well, same for you two. God, we're gonna miss you guys. Who are we supposed to complain to about the wine options now? Enjoy the Indian Ocean. We're looking forward to reading about the ocean crossing in your email updates," said Hugh, "we're sad to see you go, but like all good sailors we have to say 'see you later'." We had spent the best part of the last year sailing through Indonesia, Singapore and Malaysia with Jack and Zdenka, it felt strange saying goodbye to them as our sailing plans sent us in completely different directions.

"Fair winds." said Jack using the customary cruising good luck line.
"Fair winds to you too." said Hugh as he shook Jack's hand before Jack stepped onto their boat *Kite*.
"We'll see you again you know. Maybe in Maine hey?" said Jack.

Hugh nodded as he and I linked arms around each other's waists on the dock while Jack and Zdenka made final preparations to leave their slip. Theirs was a beautiful boat that they had had made to order in the United States six years before, the two realising their dream and seeing a boat come to life from drawings on plans. That was a once-in-a-lifetime opportunity for most of us cruisers, to design your dream boat. But today was a hard moment for us, *Kite* was sailing west to South Africa while we were sailing east to Australia via Borneo, our final goodbye after almost a year of sailing in and out of each others lives as we enjoyed the experiences Asia had for us. We grabbed their dock lines and threw them onboard as they revved the motor and started slowly pulling out of their slip. Waving a slow goodbye, Hugh hugged me closer.

The weather window looked good for their departure. The planning and discussions on the best time to leave and the best route for the sail out of Malaysia onto the wild Indian Ocean had dominated the last month of our time together here at the Johor marina. And it wasn't just *Kite* that was leaving, our friends Jake and Jackie on their boat *Hokulea* and Bill on his boat *Solstice* were leaving in a convoy, bound together as they made their final legs home to the US.

It was way back in our first days in the marina in Sydney that we had met Bill who sailed his boat *Solstice* single-handed. He had sailed in company with Jake and Jackie on *Hokulea* from California across the Pacific. It turned out that Jake and Bill were mates from their University days in Virginia and they had previously co-owned a boat and sailed it from Los Angeles to Fiji and back in a year. That was the trip that planted the seed that they should sail the world and it set in motion a seven-year plan to work hard, save money, buy boats and leave for their adventure of a lifetime.

Saying goodbye, it was always the hardest part of sailing. The relationships we formed were quick and sometimes we would meet people once or sometimes they would become an ingrained part of our lives. It was with Jack and Zdenka, Jake and Jackie and with Bill that we formed these deeper relationships as we had sailed together on and off since leaving Sydney. Meeting people out here cruising, we didn't have the usual inhibitions like in normal life. People dropped their guard and we would bond over shared hardships like the sailing conditions while enjoying a cheap sundowner beer from the local store. There was no point trying to be someone you were not, as your true self shines sooner or later when you have nothing to hide behind.

Some of the more experienced cruisers we met would talk about how they knew more about the bloke in the boat anchored next to them that they met last week than they did about their neighbour at home who they had known for ten years or more. That was because we all shared the same lifestyle and everyone was out here for their own reasons. Because we were on an extended vacation, we didn't have the same time pressures that normal land life creates like work and family commitments. There was a lot of spare time to spend relaxing and enjoying other people's company when you arrived in a place. There was the usual starting point of the bonding discussions like 'how long have you been out here?', 'where are you going?' which inevitably leads to 'why are you out here?'. Sure, not everyone was keen on telling their whole life story, but after time at sea most people are gagging to talk to other humans and people other than those who they live with on the boat – those conversations are exhausted!

The people we met also had funny ways to manage the unusual cruiser lifestyle. Like with a wonderful Australian couple that we met while sailing in Indonesia. Peter was in his seventies and Helane was in her sixties. They had sailed around the world twice before, on two different trips with two sons on their boat *Velella 3* that they had painstakingly built from scratch in the Victorian bush. They had so much to teach us from their decades of experience on the sea and I dubbed Helane my 'sailing mum'. One night aboard their boat Helane was cooking up a feast for us to share for dinner and was recounting a story.

"We had to be creative with the dinner menu. It's not easy keeping two boys interested while sailing. So we had this one dish, it got rolled out quite frequently. We called it sausage surprise." said Helane.
"Uh huh". I nodded, "sounds like a dinner with sausage in it."
"Well, that was the surprise", she said smiling. "sometimes there was no sausage."
I couldn't contain my laughter.
"You just have to make do with boat dinners sometimes, when we were at sea for four weeks at a time we wouldn't exactly have access to meat." she said.

But Helane gave me so much more, she showed me her numerous books that she had made up of their previous journeys, photos and elaborate descriptions of observations. She told me to write. To keep note of the smallest details, it was her who inspired me to write articles for magazines and share the adventure with others. Not only did it give my mind something to do on the boat, but it taught me to take more notice of the things we were doing and seeing and find ways to engage with the locals.

The other cruisers we met were from all walks of life – engineers, lawyers, bankers, doctors, builders and tradies. People with their own life story and usually people who have worked hard and have been yearning for their retirement on the water for decades. The deepening of relationships and interactions was also for those you share a boat with. Living in a confined space brings a depth to your relationship that some people don't get over a lifetime of marriage. Like Joe and his wife Anne, who we met in Thailand where the pair were beginning their new cruising life together.

"You know, my wife here – Anne, we've been married for 30 years, we have kids together," started Joe, "but they're all grown up now. We just started cruising, you know we have been out here for about a year now. It's so nice to be here like this, we spend all day together, we talk. Sometimes it feels like we never used to talk. I was working so hard and it felt like we barely saw each other." He looked over and grabbed Anne's hand.

"It's a different life on a boat, but a nice change from the life we used to live." Anne said.

"I have fallen in love with my wife all over again since we have been out here," Joe gazed lovingly at Anne and squeezed her hand. "It's just such a shame that it took us until our retirement to get to spend this time together, I feel like we know each other more deeply. Now you two, you two have the right idea, you have to keep doing this before you are too old to really enjoy it. I bloody wish I had had the idea to do this when I was younger." said Joe.

Time, it is almost limitless on a boat, everything moves so slowly. Such a contrast to normal life where other activities, deadlines and obligations fill up your day. The availability of time means that you can talk about everything and nothing, you can ponder the engineering marvels that enable a boat to float and your unresolved feelings about stars and how they impact your moods. Being a cruiser gives you a freedom to think about things differently while you travel and meet new people and make new friends.

CHAPTER THIRTEEN

Pirates!

"Pirates? What are you talking about? Aren't they mainly off Africa?" I asked Hugh.

"Nope. Says here that the waters off Sabah in Borneo is a hotspot for Filipino extremists to kidnap Malaysian locals and now foreign tourists for ransom". Hugh read off an internet page.

"What are we going to do? They're right on our path home."

"Yeah, and they have a particular interest in storming the tourist centres on the east coast of the Sabah region and killing staff and tourists to make a point. You know that dive spot that is world renowned?"

"You mean Sipadan? You know that I would love to go diving there."

"Well we can't. It's part of the disputed territories of this group and the Malaysian government. Apparently it was once Filipino land and the Abu Sayyaf militant group are fighting to get it back by terrorising the people that live in these places. They are even holding westerners to ransom by hiding them in the Philippine jungle for up to a year, and that's if they don't kill them instead."

"God, that's awful. And what are our alternatives?" I asked, nibbling on my nails.

"Well I think there are two. Neither of them is great," he paused, "one is to turn around and go south and then east through Indonesia, basically backtracking the way we have just travelled. The conditions will be poor and we will probably motor most of the way."

"And the second?"

"To sail north and go through the centre of the Philippines and across the Pacific Ocean. The conditions won't be great and it will be a long trip, about one and a half months at sea."

"What?!" I exclaimed. The mere thought of spending that long at sea got my stomach churning.

Hugh was watching the colour drain from my face, he knew that that much time at sea was a long time, especially for me.

It was 14 months into our journey and we were on the northern tip of Borneo and trying to plan our next steps. Trying to get home. The journey was always going to be a tough one but the added element of piracy was really upping the ante.

We spent the next three weeks finding all the information that we could about the pirate risk in northern Borneo. It seemed that the Abu Sayyaf Group had a drive for an Islamic republic state in the eastern Philippines, separating it from the mostly Christian country and also a land rights claim for the north of Borneo. In response, the Malaysian government set up the East Sabah Security Command in mid-2013 as a collaboration between the police, Armed Forces and Maritime Enforcement Agency to create a super department to tackle the issue of kidnapping and invasion in the Malaysian areas close to the Philippine islands. The area covered by the security command is large, not densely populated and there is a lot of water to patrol. There had been events of mass killings, executions of the general public and kidnappings which had been on the rise and culminated in an invasion of a small Malaysian fishing village in 2013 where 70 people were killed in a skirmish between local police and the Abu Sayyaf group. I felt uneasy reading about the seriousness of the situation and the increasing brazenness of the attacks by the rebel group that was not being prevented by the Malaysian Authorities.

The pirate risk had escalated in the recent months while we had been sailing around Malaysia and was getting more attention in the expat press and online sailing forums. The most recent case had involved two German cruisers being plucked from their yacht near the disputed waters and taken to an unknown location in some jungle in the Philippines.

Hugh and I kept talking about sailing options, how we could get home in the best time and best conditions possible.

"What if we run the gauntlet? What if we sail over Borneo past these guys but just don't stop?" I asked Hugh, tapping my fingers on the table.

"No way. There's no way. The risk is so high. The reason why it's happening here, apart from the politics and poverty of the situation, is that the distance between the Malaysian land and the Filipino land is only 20 miles. 20 miles! That's so close. If you are kidnapped from your boat that's it, you're trapped in remote jungle with people that just see a dollar sign above your head."

I shook my head, the whole concept of being kidnapped was just so frightening.

"It's a terrible risk, you just have to think that what if they are there and waiting for people like us? They can outrun us so easy." said Hugh. "They use small boats with powerful outboard engines that go up to four times the speed of our miserly seven knot speed. And that's if we were running the engine at full power, we would be no match for them." Hugh paused to see my reaction and could see the disappointment in my face and took my hand. "I have thought about this a million ways, they could damage the boat or hurt us and I couldn't bear it if you were hurt. I'm not going to do it, we can't sail that way, we have to pick another way." he pulled me in close and I could tell it was something that had been worrying him.

"So you have even thought about how we would protect ourselves if there is a threat?" I asked.

"Yeah, I reckon I would get the flare gun. While it isn't like a normal gun, shooting someone or a small boat with a lit flare would be a good technique. If nothing else, it would get them scrambling from the shock of a bright lit thing landing in their boat. But that is it really, we don't have the water cannon guns that the big cargo ships use to deter pirates coming aboard."

After that conversation we focused on the other sailing route options. I really didn't like either of the sailing options that Hugh had presented as we would be spending a lot of time at sea and working hard against bad conditions like swell and wind. Being on a sailing boat exposes you in the most primitive way to the changes in the seasons and can make a trip long and absolutely miserable if the conditions were opposing you. The other terrifying risk of sailing through the Philippines was the looming typhoon season which was just about to start. If we were to go that route we put ourselves at risk of being caught in a typhoon which brings strong wind of up to 100 knots and high seas. Only two years prior typhoon Haiyan had struck the eastern group of Philippine islands and combined with a tsunami wave killed 6,300 people. We could be putting ourselves at serious risk, and there would only be a few days warning about where a typhoon is predicted to go and by then we could be stuck in the typhoon hotspot.

"Where can we go? Our options are to go back through Indonesia or north through the Philippines." Hugh said and we talked again about routing options. "I have been searching the internet for sailors writing about which way they went and how the conditions were for them, lots of Aussies go back through Indonesia to Darwin."
"And then what?" I asked.
"Exactly, it's hard to get the boat back to Sydney from Darwin, the weather windows to go east travelling to Cairns are short and the best time is right in the middle of cyclone season at Christmas."
"You are really convincing me with this one." I said sarcastically.
"I know, it's not even an option really. But I did talk to those Aussie cruisers at the dock the other day and they had done the trip before where they sailed across the top of the Indonesian islands then hopped down the Papua New Guinea Coast after going through the Pacific Ocean from Borneo. We could do that one, but again the conditions

down the New Guinea coast aren't good, the wind is fluky and there is strong current against. But we can set out for it and just be prepared for a hard slog down the coast. It's an easy hop from New Guinea to Cairns from there. That's the one."

"The options are miserable. Should we just leave the boat here when we are done and fly home?"

"No way! I am not leaving the boat here to die. Which is what will happen in this heat and humidity. Plus I do really want to bring her home, you know, complete the journey."

"It's a lot of work just to feel good about bringing the boat home."

"It's not just about bringing her home. It is finishing. Leaving the boat is easy."

"You don't always have to take the hard road you know."

"Don't be so patronising. This is the adventure we set out for." Hugh said as he walked up the companionway to the cockpit.

We weren't going to solve this one today. Either way we go it seemed our east bound trip was going to be epic because it was a long way to go. And a long way to go 'the wrong way'. The direction that the wind and currents move are crucial to route planning especially when the passage could be so long and would likely make our journey even longer.

A few more days passed and while we were not talking about sailing routes, Hugh was constantly on the computer looking at maps and reading reviews of sailing conditions to help make his decision about which way to go. The route through the Philippines started to become his favoured one as the east-bound conditions through the Pacific historically had more wind to get us closer to home. The alternate route through Indonesia would likely be far less sailing and more motoring as the winds would be directly on the nose and the adverse conditions would be strengthening as the days ticked by and the season settled into its usual trade-wind pattern.

There were lots of ways we could collect data and information on previous years, but the predictions for the upcoming season required educated guesswork. Having been sailing through Asia for a year now, Hugh was becoming a bit of a wind whisperer, understanding the signs, knowing the history and the patterns of weather. He was using a handful of websites and apps to see how the weather predictions were a culmination of historical data, local anomalies and updates based on low or high pressure systems moving through the region. Hours he spent up on deck just watching the clouds or the sky change colour and he would start to note what time things happened during the day and mentally record the sequences of how conditions changed and catalogue them for future use.

Using the information from the internet and some mapping information he started to plot how our sail could go and the different options we had for making it east in the best possible time. He was keen for us to not get stuck in the doldrums bobbing around in the northern Pacific Ocean for months which was the real risk with the Philippine route that he was favouring.

"I have it." Hugh said one day with a gleeful smile.
"Have what?" I asked tentatively.
"I know the trip we are going to take."
"Uh-huh."
"So we go from Kudat, here", he said as he pointed to the map on his computer screen.
I came closer and bent over his shoulder, Kudat was the next town we were due to dock at and it was on the north-western tip of Borneo. "Then we go north up the western side of the Philippines, on the outside of the islands there, we need to put as much water between us and the kidnapping Filipino's." he turned to look at me trying to gauge my response.
I looked blankly at the screen, "so what's next after leaving Borneo?"
"Once we get to the top of the Palawan island we go east, threading our way through the islands of the Philippines. There are so many you see." he gestured towards the thousands of islands on his screen as he zoomed out. "So we only have a few weeks to get through, there are some

good typhoon holes in case we need to get shelter from a coming storm. That was how I picked the route."

"Okay, it sounds good." I said.

"Then we can go from there to Palau."

"Oooh, Palau. I saw some pictures of Palau, looks amazing."

"Loads of good diving. We can also use it to stock up on boat and food supplies."

"Stock up?" I asked.

"After Palau we have some big water to cross, we have to go across the Pacific Ocean to the Solomon Islands or Papua New Guinea, I haven't quite got that bit sorted."

"How much water are you talking about?"

"It would be like 2000 nautical miles from Palau to the Solomons." Hugh turned to see my eyes go big and the smile drop from my face. "That's between 20-30 days at sea for that part of the journey."

I walked a few steps away and sat down on the settee. I put my head in my hands and tried to grapple with the idea. I was so intimidated by spending that much time at sea and being completely remote and alone with the elements. Hugh came and sat next to me, putting his arm around me and rubbing my shoulder as he pulled me towards him in a comforting hug.

We decided to go north and through the Philippines, the journey would take us through the centre of the Philippine archipelago and then east across the Pacific Ocean to the island nation of Palau. The plan from there was to stay north of Papua New Guinea because the strait heading east along its coast was notorious for opposing winds and current. You would probably start to head the wrong way because the current can be so strong. So we could try and stay north and drop down to turn south just above the Solomon Islands. From there we would be able to keep an easy southerly route to north Queensland on the Australian east coast. We now had a basic plan to get home and avoid the pirated waters. The daunting part was the 4500 nautical miles we had to travel to do this route to get to Queensland, it was significantly further than we had previously planned, but I felt like we needed to go this way now and we had to commit.

CHAPTER FOURTEEN

Palau

The sail from the Philippines to Palau was hard. Hard because we were leaving in difficult sailing conditions - in the aftermath of a typhoon system that had just passed to the north. Hard because it was the start of our Pacific Ocean crossing. And hard because we didn't really know what lay ahead of us. We were starting the east bound leg, sailing uphill, trying to come home from South East Asia via a route rarely taken. It was 16 months into our trip and we started to feel like we were on the journey home.

35 knot southerly winds blasted us for four days, intense rain fell from a grey sky for three of those days. The boat

was heeled forcefully by the wind and was hammered by four metre waves that crashed over the side of the boat and drenched the main sail. The whole boat was covered in a salty crystalline shell, my skin stung from the salt that was embedded in my blistered and callused hands.

Finally on our fifth day of the crossing, the world suddenly looked brighter. The wind was steadily dropping, below 25kts and the seas reduced to under two metres. We rubbed our salt encrusted eyes as the sun shone brilliantly and it was one of those perfect days at sea. Later its beauty faded when Hugh realised as he started the engine to charge the batteries that the engine was overheating. Hugh looked over at me with a worried expression on his face.
"What?" I asked him.
"We might have to give Palau a miss if I can't fix this." he said.
I looked down at the sole of the cockpit. He knew I had been really looking forward to going there, not only for the break in the sailing, but it was considered one of the world's most premier dive sites.
"I'm going to do everything I can to fix it, but I am not confident enough to sail through that reef entry, it's 15 nautical miles long and we will be spotting with our eyes the whole time, we can't sail it." he explained.

Hugh put his head torch on and submerged himself in the engine bay and got to work pulling the engine and water cooling system apart. I remained in the cockpit and hand steered the boat to reduce the draw on the batteries by the auto-pilot. Without the engine to charge the batteries we would run out of power quickly. Due to the strong winds, the boat was still heeling heavily to port and we were receiving knocking waves, I felt for Hugh who was lying across the main engine in the cramped engine bay being pounded by the rough seas.

The hours ticked by, the sun set and the moon shone brightly above. Hugh systematically went through the process of dismantling the water cooling system.
"How are you going in there?" I asked Hugh as he wearily came up to the cockpit for some fresh air.
"Slowly. I removed the cooling water impeller and discovered it had shed four blades, now the hunt is on for the rubber fragments that were lost. They could be anywhere in any of the myriad of segments of the engine hoses." he said. His shoulders were hunched and his face and body were covered in black stripes of engine grease. Trying to repair the engine at sea in the tough conditions was taking its toll on the usually unflappable Hugh. "Those shredded bits of rubber could be lodged anywhere along the water piping system and blocking the cooling water from getting to the engine to cool it." he continued, "I'll just have to open the heat exchanger and hopefully the pieces will be in there. If they are not, I don't know where to look next."

"Look, it's 2am, do you want to have a rest?" I asked him as I ducked down to the galley and passed him a cold cordial drink.

"No, I just have to do this one bit. Keep steering and I'll come up after I try the exchanger." he said, before gulping down his drink and returning down below.

Hugh was gone for another few hours problem-solving in the engine bay. Finally after opening the last piece of the cooling system - the lube oil cooler, he found where the rubber had lodged itself, blocking the cooling engine water network. Almost 24 hours after finding the problem, a hot, tired and very relieved Hugh collapsed into bed for some sleep. We were going to make Palau after all.

The following day was our last day at sea and Hugh spotted Palau, "land-ho!" he cried. The hazy green rising land form was visible on the horizon, spotted 15 nautical miles off the bow and in perfect conditions of bright sunshine and favourable winds. The wind had dropped to 15 knots, so we unfurled our big jib sail, excited by the prospect of making landfall that day. As we approached the reef-ringed entry channel Hugh started up the engine and beamed that it was running well and the cooling system was working perfectly. I stood up on the bow and spotted the entry, directing to Hugh who was sitting in the cockpit hand steering the boat. The reefs we were navigating gave off a brilliant array of aqua colours from miles away, the water was a pale blue and its clarity was spectacular. It was the sight we had been longing to see and it was very exciting to be arriving in a new country. The water was so clear and I could see the coral formations on the sea bed below. The entry was shallow at between three and ten metres, so I was tensely pacing the deck to try to see the obstacles in our path to accurately guide the boat through.

Before leaving the Philippines we had read about the place to anchor in Palau, it was outside a dive company called Sam's Dive Tours which doubled as the home of the Royal Palau Yacht Club. Sam – the guy who ran the company, was a US expat who now lived in Palau with his Palauan wife and kids. The club was renowned amongst cruisers as a great place to relax, enjoy some food and beers while hanging out with other cruisers and retelling old sea tales.

After spending three hours slowly weaving through the reef entry we made our way to the lagoon and dropped anchor outside the dive shop. It was so refreshing to drop the sails, turn off the engine and sit on deck to take in the surrounds of our new temporary home. Hugh opened a bottle of red wine and poured us both a glass. I fell into Hugh's embrace as we soaked up the view and the dimming of the light as the sun started to fade behind the rock formations that encircled our little lagoon.

He tipped his glass towards mine "well, here's to completing the first 550 nautical miles of our east bound leg." he said.

"Cheers." I said and I chinked his glass with mine. The passage had been rough and we were covered in bruises from being bumped around on the boat. The silence of the boat being still was what we both desperately needed, a chance to relax and have a decent sleep.

We used the next few days to recuperate from the sailing. A few things on the boat needed minor repairs, so Hugh set about on his customary trips to the hardware and paint stores, the supermarket and anywhere else that had the parts he needed. We also indulged in some scuba diving trips with Sam's Tours.

We didn't know much about Palau before it became a destination for us, so we read up on the place, finding brochures or historical plaques about the island. We knew details about its location - that it was a remote island nation, 550 nautical miles from the Philippines and 400 nautical miles from Guam. One brochure detailed that 'the native people on the land originated from Indonesia and other nearby Micronesian islands or the Philippines.' It went on to explain how 'throughout the last 300 years the Spanish had colonised the islands but subsequently lost them to the United States after the American-Spanish War of 1898. Then it was barely 20 years later when the

Japanese started their expansion policy in the Pacific and overran the islands to use them for mining, fishing and coconut plantations. During World War II the country became one of the Pacific's theatres of war between the USA and Japan, bringing bombings and bloody battles on the islands. Ultimately when the USA won the war in 1944, there was a significant cultural change for the country from being Japanese speakers and eating Japanese food, to learning English, using the US dollar and driving on the right-hand side of the road.'

A few days in Palau turned into a few weeks and we were becoming regulars at the bar at Sam's Place. It was a dive shop by day, which saw hundreds of people coming and going on various boat tours out to the reefs. The place then transformed into a casual bar by night, with delicious fresh sushi dishes, hamburgers and fried chicken being offered in a Palauan cultural food fusion accompanied by cold beer and wine. The bar was almost always full of boisterous drinking and cruisers telling yarns of near misses and epic sailing adventures. The bar was lined with large timber tables and bench seating on a concrete floor. The building was formed by one side wall and had two open sides, so you could see out to the small lagoon harbour and watch the sunset and the anchored boats lightly swaying as the tide changed direction. The building design allowed the cooling evening breeze to sweep through the bar and bring relief from the hot muggy days that the tropical weather brought. On the odd occasion when the place was not full, you could sit at the bar stools and chit-chat with the Filipino bar staff and listen to the tropical rain pound the corrugated iron roof above.

One night we had already been at the bar for a few hours drinking beers when cruisers Bob and Dave started talking about a magical place in the Pacific Ocean, a tiny atoll called Kapingamarangi, a group of islands where the people lived remotely and self-sufficiently amongst palms and pristine waters. It sounded like an island paradise. They talked about the place wistfully with longing in their voices.

"Oh yeah, I have been wanting go there ever since I heard about it." started Dave.
"Do you know anyone who has made it there?" I asked.
"Well, sometimes you hear someone at the bar in Hawaii or here in Palau who has used it as a respite stop while crossing the Pacific, but it is quite far south and would make the eastbound leg hard. You have to go against the wind to get back out of it and up north enough to get back on the rhum line from Hawaii." Dave answered.
"So do you know it even exists?" I asked.
"Of course it exists, it is part of Micronesia! Pohnpei is the capital but it's a long way from there, the atoll is 500 nautical miles south of Pohnpei. It's much easier to sail to

Pohnpei and still stay on the sailing line than dip south to Kapingamarangi." said Bob.

"Us cruisers always dream of visiting those islands where the people live a traditional way of life. A life that didn't get completely ruined by the missionaries imposing a different god and changing the customs of the places. A god that requires them to cover their women or be ashamed of their bodies." said Dave with a wistful look in his eyes.

"Some of the islands were saved, like, they were driving themselves along a path of self-destruction, you know with cannibalism and savagery." said Bob.

"But the missionaries changed their history, their traditions. I just don't accept that they made it better for the people. I do dream of going back a couple of hundred years and just experiencing those islands, seeing what life was like before the west came in and meddled." said Dave.

"But Kapingamarangi is said to be almost completely self-sufficient. They only eat what they can grow or catch. I don't know what the people are like though, I have never been there." said Bob.

Hugh leaned in, he was very interested in a potential respite stop for our long passage.

"So do you have any waypoints for where this place is or the reef entry?" asked Hugh.

"Yeah, I do have some, but you have to take these things with a grain of salt, if you hit the reef out there you are stuffed. You won't have any access to repairs or spares. It would be the end of your trip, there is no way you could sail out of there with a broken boat." said Bob.

This was an invitation for Hugh, the more exciting, remote and exotic sounding the better. It started him off on a treasure hunt to see what he could find about the place and put it on our route planning so we could go if we needed a break or needed to sit out some bad weather. It would be 1200 nautical miles to Kapingamarangi, at least 12 days at sea. Hugh began furiously researching the atoll, the conditions and the historical weather patterns. If we were to go to the atoll, or even in the direction of it, it meant staying on a sailing line a lot further north than we had previously planned, we would not go to Papua New Guinea after all and then continue to sail further east over the top of the Solomon Islands instead.

One of the things we had become used to while cruising was the hit-and-miss opportunities to get internet, so doing research was at times an intensive task. Communications on Palau was a big challenge because of its remoteness and small population. The internet was woefully slow and expensive to use. There was one internet company on the island and it used satellite dishes to connect to a dial up modem. Hugh would go to the internet café and sit for hours on an incredibly slow connection tediously drawing small pieces of information about Kapingamarangi to put together his info pack.

He eventually found some small details about the Atoll: "Hey, come listen to this." Hugh touched my arm to bring me over and read me the page he found. "'Kapingamarangi Atoll is 600 nautical miles from the nearest population centre and is inhabited by a pocket of Polynesians who had drifted 1500 miles from the eastern Pacific Ocean on handmade canoes sometime in the 1600s. It is the most remote and isolated island in the West Pacific, there are no airport, roads or cars.'"

"Wow, it's so different to places we have been, it sounds like it is a place stuck in time. I wonder if they even like having people like us visit." I said.

"Mmm. I do wonder if we do more harm than good by coming in with our modern boat to a place that wouldn't have access to half the things we do. But then, maybe they get excited by someone new coming." said Hugh.

"Oh, here is another page," I said as I clicked through another link. "'The race by European countries for more land brought the Spaniards to Kapingamarangi who claimed it theirs around the same time as staking claim in the Caroline Islands and the Philippines. Those island nations all got traded after the US-Spanish War, when the US gave it to the Germans. It was consequently taken by the Japanese in 1914 when Japan was on a Pacific nation land grab. After the defeat of Japan in World War Two, and like so many of the islands in the Pacific Ocean, it fell under the jurisdiction of the United States as a Trust Territory of the Pacific Islands and was supported by the

US for some food support, aid money and infrastructure investment.'" I read.

"What a tumultuous 200 years it's had." said Hugh. "It really sounds like an interesting place. This one is definitely going on the list of potential stopping points."

I was quite excited about the opportunity of a rest stop on our passage, but equally aware that it was only a possibility because all good sailing plans can become unstuck for one reason or another.

The other thing that Hugh was researching were weather details for the upcoming passages. He found that the US organisation – the National Oceanic and Atmospheric Administration captured information via satellite imagery and ocean temperature data which showed the longitude of what was called the 'east-flowing counter current' – a stretch of water that moved opposite to the constant west flowing current in this part of the Pacific. The counter current moved at up to four knots and would give us extra speed to cover the long distance. The challenge was finding the current as it moved around seasonally, so you could sail for days trying to find it and then miss it completely. Hugh was also looking at weather data and historical typhoon path data from previous years and knew that we needed to get ready to leave Palau soon as the season was changing and typhoons would be becoming more likely the longer we waited.

What we thought was going to be a couple of weeks turned into a month stay in Palau, the extent of our visa. Hugh had found a weather window which had some strong conditions initially, but which calmed over about seven days. The strong conditions would provide us with solid wind to make some good miles on what would be our biggest passage yet.

CHAPTER FIFTEEN

'To Carry Under the Arms of the Sky'

Twelve days at sea, I never thought that I could have survived such a long time out in the big blue. We didn't see any signs of human life; no boats, planes, islands, nothing. Just us and the water and the boat. The start of the sail was exhausting as we had experienced strong and steady winds and huge downpours of rain, so much rain that the boat was leaking waterfalls and some of our electronics got irreparably wet. But we made it through that and the end of the sail was marked with beautiful sunny days, some delicious fish we caught off the back of the boat with the fishing line we were trawling and ideal conditions for attempting to enter a reef-encircled atoll.

The timing of our arrival at the atoll was perfect as it was the middle of the day, bright and sunny and so we decided to attempt the entry. We could see the waves crashing over the reef ahead as the ocean met with it and broke the waves. The sound of the water hitting the reef was so loud, and such a contrast to our last few days sailing in light winds, that I sat in the cockpit of the boat drumming my fingers on the sideboard as we approached. Hugh stood on the bow with binoculars trying to spy the entry point through the reef. The entry was not mapped and we were relying on what we saw to make it through without damaging the boat. The entry was through a narrow gap in the reef wall that had developed naturally by the volume of water passing through with changing tides. Hugh had located the point and came back to the cockpit to start to steer towards it. It was tricky and I had moved up to the bow to spot for Hugh while he steered the boat, having heart palpitations as we drew nearer because the water was so shallow and clear. I could see the detail in the coral formations below which appeared much closer than they were. Because Hugh was sitting in the cockpit he couldn't see what lay directly ahead of the bow, so he was blind to the obstacles ahead. I used arm and hand signals to indicate where the sea floor looked too shallow. But I was also constantly asking him what the depth indicator read.

I used my right hand to show Hugh to move to starboard. "What is the depth?" I yelled over the noise of the engine.

"It's four meters, we're fine." Hugh responded.
"But it looks like it's getting shallower." I said, bouncing from one foot to the other up at the bow of the boat.
"It's ok, it's steady at four meters."
"It's just so clear, it's so hard to see how deep it really is."
"It's ok, just keep your eyes on bommies up ahead." He said as he warned me to look out for coral heads that we would have to steer around.
We nervously crossed the shallow and narrow entry point and breathed out a shared breath as we slowly steered through.

Once we were past the entry we could see the line of islands on the far side of the lagoon, it seemed to be about six miles away, though we were not quite sure which one was where the villagers lived as there were a row of islands covered in dense palm trees and it could have been any one of them.

It took about an hour to get from the lagoon entry to closer to the palm-covered islands across the water that was clear and flat, protected inside the reef wall. While we were busy making our way across the lagoon, a local man zoomed up in his small outboard powered boat to welcome us and point us in the direction of the Touhou islet and main village. We were very close so we continued a little further west and found a good spot to anchor on the sandy bottom.

We dropped anchor and then had to go through the diplomatic process of seeking the Chief - Alpino Samuels' permission to stay for a few days. The Chief was delivered to our boat by the local man who had just given us directions for anchoring. They were in what turned out to the atoll's only fiberglass boat with an outboard engine. Alpino was a short man, maybe five foot seven, he had a large belly and dark brown skin and despite just wearing a t-shirt and cargo shorts he was the Chief of the island and ultimately responsible for law and order here. He looked to be in his fifties and was a reserved man. We invited him on board and he stepped up bringing a big bunch of coconuts as a gift which we graciously accepted. We all sat in the cockpit in the shade.

"Where do you come from?" Alpino asked.

"From Palau, we have sailed for 12 days and 12 nights." answered Hugh.

"And you have visa? You have been to Pohnpei?" asked Alpino.

"No, we have not been to Pohnpei, we wanted to ask you if we could stay for a few days as we have some things to fix on our boat." said Hugh. I could sense the nervousness in Hugh's body language as he looked intently at Alpino to gauge his reaction. We didn't know if we would be welcomed here and we were uncertain whether they would let us stay, we hoped that because they were such an outlying island so far from the main island of Pohnpei that they would let us stay.

"You need permit to stay here." said Alpino.

"Maybe we can stay for a very short time. We will be no trouble." said Hugh.

"Well, you can stay for just few days, to fix boat, then if you want to stay longer you have to go Pohnpei." said Alpino.

"Oh thank you, yes we will only be a few days." said Hugh.

Alpino seemed to relax a bit now that we had discussed our business. We brought up some gifts as an offering including some reading glasses, fish hooks and cans of spam. His eyes lit up with the spam and glasses and he tried to hide a smile. We had heard from many other cruisers that we should bring basic essentials like clothing, fishing line and hooks, reading glasses, paper and pencils as well as food gifts to these outlying islands as they rarely received supplies and these are the sorts of things that can really improve their lives.

"So are there any rascals that we need to be aware of?" asked Hugh, sounding Alpino out for advice about whether we should be careful of anyone here.

"Some men, they sit down by the water, they drink too much. But everyone else, they are a quiet people." said Alpino. It seemed that he kept the community in order and we would be safe while visiting here, that was a relief.

Alpino did not want to stay and make small talk. He said goodbye and got back in his boat and zoomed back off toward the pier at the village. A refreshing wind blew off the water as Hugh and I relaxed back into the cockpit seats. This place was amazing and so beautiful, we couldn't believe our luck that we had managed to enter such a little known about place in what felt like the middle of the Pacific Ocean with no other life in coo-ee and with a Chief happy to let us stay, albeit for just a few days.

The whole lagoon was protected by a ring of small uninhabited islands that were either covered in dense jungle or were just small sandy bumps rising above the water, and there must have been about 30 of them, and then there was the main island. The locals lived on the main island for obvious reasons, it was the highest above sea level – and offered the greatest protection from wave surges and storms, even though it was barely one and a half meters above sea level, it was the best of the lot.

It was late in the day and Hugh and I were tired from our journey and the excitement of the day and settled back with some rum drinks. As nighttime fell glimmers of pink in the sky disappeared to give way to a canopy of stars; the island fell silent and all we could hear was the low hum of a generator driving electricity for lights in only three places - the church, the primary school and the chief's office. A bell was rung at 8:30pm to mark the end of the day and a shroud of silence fell over the place and those few electric lights were turned off. A few fires flickered on shore from the remnants of dinner cooking and the sound of the crashing waves on the outer reef was all we could hear. It was hard to explain my emotions of surviving that length of time at sea and to be safe in this breathtaking location, it was a mixture of relief, accomplishment and a little bit of shared pride. But our exhaustion overtook us and for the first time and in almost two weeks we slept for longer than the three hours afforded to us during our night shift pattern that we had to adopt when we were sailing overnight.

The next morning I had to rub my eyes to remember where we were and that it wasn't just a dream. We were roused by the ringing of the bell at 6:30am and the beaming sunshine.

After a slow breakfast aboard, we got our things together to set out to explore the island; we were absolutely sick of being on the boat and desperately wanted to go for a walk on solid ground. We dingied into shore to find dozens of kids frolicking in the water and jumping off the pier, the best splash got the biggest hoops and cheers from the on-looking children. We walked along the concrete pier and there we were in the village, with a concrete church just a few hundred meters in front of us and a number of huts either side. We could see that there was a giant brass bell captured in an arch-like structure at the front of the church building, this seemed to be the bell for signaling the end and start of the day. The huts surrounding us were made of various parts of the palm tree. They had a raised floor section – about one metre off the ground supported by palm tree beams and layered with strong palm leaf weaved bedding. The roof was also made of palm tree beams and layers of palm leaves and the roofing was at such steep angles and the leaves hung down so low you had to bend down to see who was sitting in the hut. This low angled roof provided protection from the direct sun and rain but still allowed the cooling evening wind to blow through and take out the heat of the day. We could see people sitting in there either working, doing food preparation, or sleeping. The other type of house was from a design that must have been influenced by western culture as they were concrete walled buildings with dirt floors and a tiled or metal roof. We could see they were used to store the cooking implements and clothes but also provide shelter when the weather was very nasty. You couldn't miss these houses, they were bright and warm, painted with brilliant orange, blue or lime green colours which were in stark contrast to the deep green of the surrounding palm trees.

While walking through the village we could see that everyone was busy. The women were weaving palm leaves into various useful items like baskets, mats, seats and replacement flooring for the houses. The men were doing building work. One of the houses needed new palm leaf roofing, so there were a number of men hollering to each other while clambering around on the roof of a hut. There was another group of young teenagers who were sitting around in a circle and making copra – shredding the flesh from the inside of a coconut. The way that they did it was fascinating to watch. They sat on a metal seat which had a protruding arm with a sharp round cutter that was between their legs and on this arm they rolled and rotated the centre of the open coconut. The shredded coconut then fell into a bucket below the protruding arm and it was routinely emptied onto large tarpaulin sheets and dried. Copra was the only export from this island and the only money-making enterprise; it was used in soaps, cosmetics and food.

The locals were very reserved, their demeanor was something we had not come across in our travels and they seemed to shy away from us as we passed. We thought back to Sulewesi in Indonesia where we were mobbed for photos like rock stars, and generally overwhelmed by the intrigue they showed. This was a very different experience as while they may have been interested in why we were here, they kept to themselves and left us wondering if we had offended them or worse; were we breaking the rules by being there?

The other thing that was obvious was the tidiness of the place. Paths had been made connecting the huts and the plots of food growing gardens together. They were neatly swept dirt with small rocks placed at the edges. We could see that the people had a strong civic pride and wanted their village to be neat and tidy; there was no rubbish to be seen and their belongings were kept stacked and tidy. We walked down one path, we didn't know where we were going but after so many trips to new places we were used to just going for walks to see what there was to see. We walked past one of the palm tree huts and a lady was busy weaving some palm leaves together into a mat. We waved good morning to her and without saying a word she stopped us by gesturing with her hands and quickly cut open a coconut for us to drink and eat, I gratefully accepted saying 'thank you', I loved fresh coconuts.

As we continued on through the village we came to a concrete bridge that connected two of the islands. We hadn't noticed the bridge when we sailed passed, but it connected the main island of Touhou with the one next to it – Werua – where more of the village spread. There were more of the palm tree huts and concrete houses. Werua had a more dispersed layout for the houses and garden plots. The bridge was strong and about two metres wide and as we crossed it we could see some damage and huge cracks through parts of it and places where some of the supporting pylons had fallen and crashed into the shallow water below. In that shallow water some of the local kids had placed rocks that spelled out 'welcome to Kapinga'. On the other side of the bridge we could see that once again the locals were busy working and the kids were busy playing with sticks or helping their parents with chores like handwashing clothes.

But as we walked on we were stopped on the path by one of the locals, he introduced himself, his name was Sakius. He was a middle aged man with some white flecks in his dark brown hair, he looked to be about 50 and had a large belly which slightly hung down below his t-shirt and in his right hand he held a thick book which dangled down by his side. He looked over his reading glasses at us with a warm smile.
"Hi. What are you doing here? I can see your boat." he said.
"Just going for a walk. You have a beautiful island here." said Hugh. We had become used to non-English speakers sounding abrupt when they spoke and we were excited to find someone who spoke English and we could chat to.
"Yes, thank you, we love our island. Why don't you come have coffee?" he asked.
We nodded and followed him down a short dirt path to some plastic seats around a small table which was shaded by a tarpaulin held up on sticks and we stooped below the tarpaulin to sit down as he gestured with his hands.
"Do you want coffee?" he asked.
"Oh yes, I will." said Hugh.
I shook my head "no thanks, I have my coconut." I said between slurps.

Just next to where we were sitting Sakius poured hot water from a metal tea pot into two white plastic mugs and threw a heaped tablespoon of instant granules and added a huge spoon of sugar and passed one to Hugh while he kept one for himself. He sat down on the other side of the table.

"Thanks." said Hugh as he sipped the brown drink and rolled the super sweet mix around in his mouth.

"Do you have any books?" Sakius asked.

"We have many books, do you like to read?" asked Hugh.

"I like books about history, the world. I used to be a teacher you know, I like to read about other places." responded Sakius.

"You were a teacher, where did you teach?" asked Hugh.

"I taught here at Kapinga for a bit, but also at Pohnpei at the high school there. The kids go there for high school you know, they go on a boat which takes three days and then they spend four months living on Pohnpei and go to school and then come back here for four months."

"Wow, that's a long time to be without their family. Where do they live?" I asked.

"Well most of the people here have some of their family living on Pohnpei, so the kids, they stay with aunty or uncle or cousin. There is actually a village there called Kapinga, cause it's made up of the people that have left here. It's not like living here though, Pohnpei is bigger, it has the television, the internet. You don't get any of that here, it's just the island here." said Sakius.

I looked around and could imagine how different it would be there. I could hear the background sounds of the waves rolling on the reef on the other side of the island, the louder noise of the insects in the jungle and the wind lightly stirring the palm tree leaves above. I could see that Sakius lived in one of the concrete houses, it was painted a lime green with some pink trimming. Out the front of the house he had this plastic outdoor table set with another small table next to it that had a small gas camp stove that he put the metal kettle on to boil water. Next to the kettle sat a tin of instant coffee, sugar and a tin of Nestlé chocolate powder. The ground below our feet was packed dirt swept clean from leaves and sticks, and tall palm trees crowded around the small clearing. It felt like a very secluded spot, not like a busier island capital.

"I can't imagine going away for school. Some people do that where we are from, but it is not common. I suppose all the kids here on islands in the Pacific go away for school at some time." I said.

"Yes, sometimes it is further, they go to Fiji or Hawaii, maybe even the mainland of the United States, it's part of what happened at the end of World War Two." said Sakius.

"Yeah we read about some of the history of how different countries claimed ownership here. But even though so many countries said they owned this place your way of life looks close to a traditional lifestyle, is that true?". I asked.

"It is close to the traditional way, but not quite. You know we still grow taro, coconuts, bananas and breadfruit, we domesticate pigs and chickens so that we have something else to eat apart from seafood. We speak our own Polynesian language and we still use song to tell old stories and teach the children about life on Kapinga." Sakius said. "But when the Japanese ruled here they commercialised copra exportation, and the big ships come sometimes. We trade copra and get coffee or sugar in exchange. But the missionaries, they came in the 1900s, they brought their religion and made people forget our traditional tribal religion with our ruling spirits. They shamed the people into wearing clothes more than their loin cloths and we lost our singing which taught the children about the stories they need to know about the rules of life and the island." he paused. We sat in silence captured by his story and looking intently at him. "You know, I have a book you might like to read. It is about Kapingamarangi. It was written by some Americans, they studied the people here in the 1950's and wrote a book about it all. But you have to promise to bring it back, it's the only copy on the island."

"Of course." I said.

"But now I have more reading to do. Why don't you come back tomorrow? Don't forget to bring me some books."

"Okay sure, thanks." said Hugh. "Oh, I have one question, is it okay to talk to the people here? They seem shy or something – like they don't want us here."

"No, they just don't speak much English. Everyone learns English at school, but they also have a respect system where they don't speak unless spoken to. It's ok, you haven't done anything wrong."

"Okay, thanks." said Hugh as Sakius passed him the book and we waved goodbye.

When we met Sakius we had just about reached the end of the path, so we turned around to return to the centre of the village. We passed some of the small gardens and we could see some of the crops growing, the taro, herbs and breadfruit. We delicately dodged some chickens that were running around trying to evade small children that were chasing them.

We got back to the boat absorbing our island visit. We hadn't been anywhere like this on our trip so far and it was the stuff that cruisers talk about with mist in their eyes, the kind of place that is locked in time that gave us travellers a chance to visualise what life was like for islanders hundreds of years ago.

I started delving into the book that Sakius had leant us. I sat in the cockpit with a cordial drink in one hand and relaxed back leaning the large book on my legs. It was fascinating. I could not believe that 60 years after the visit of the American ethnographers who wrote the book, so much of the island's life was the same despite the rise of computer technology and the international education afforded to many of the island's children. Many of the influences of the outside world had not made it back here as there was no stable electricity nor internet. The book went through the history of the naming of the place, and found that the locals just referred to it as 'the land'. Without any visitors for hundreds of years at a time why would you need a name for your place? It made complete sense, it was just 'home'. Polynesian interpretations of the name Kapinga-marangi could be translated 'to carry under the arms' - of 'the sky'. It was a really beautiful way to see the island through their eyes and understand how they wanted to describe it. The book recounted a study done by some German ethnographers in the early 1900s where they had detailed the islander's methods for self-sufficient farming. We could see that they had pretty much the same diet and relied primarily on their own gardens for survival because a supply ship visits the island - from Pohnpei, only two or three times a year; it only brings long-life stores like rice, sugar, tea and coffee. The limited income of the islanders means that the locals live off their produce and enjoy the variety provided by outside food only occasionally. It dawned on me the excitement that the Chief must have felt when we gave him the can of spam.

The Americans found that the practice of story-telling had been virtually lost after the 1920s when Christian missionaries arrived, banning the singing of non-Christian songs, so traditional songs about marriage, custom and law, and the skills for making fabric, rope, canoes and houses had disappeared. As I was reading this book I could hear off to the side of the boat two girls in the water, I thought they were just playing and singing, but I could see that they had a small net and looked like they were fishing.

I paused to reflect on how special it was that they would sing to each other while doing their work and perhaps singing had not disappeared entirely as a cultural practice.

CHAPTER SIXTEEN

Forever

I was sitting alone on the small island just a short dingy ride from the main island of Kapingamarangi, Hugh and I had come across in the dingy as he wanted us to go snorkelling together. The texture on the ground was something I had not experienced before. It was made up of tiny white pieces of broken and old dead coral and was rough and sharp and really hard to walk on without wincing. I picked up some small pieces and examined them intently; they were full of so much detail and pock-marked with tiny shallow holes as if they had been sand blasted. The island was made up of the coral rubble and some palm trees that stood motionless on that still afternoon. No other obvious landscape features made up this tiny dot of an island.

As I sat on the rough coral I indulged in a delicious young coconut. The sweet flavour of the flesh and the thirst quenching coconut water soothed my dry mouth as I watched Hugh splashing about. He seemed to be quite fascinated by some of the coral heads. I looked over to check that the dingy was still safe floating in the water of the bay, secured with its tiny anchor on the shallow cove floor, then went back to the coconut. I could eat those all day.

Hugh gestured for me to come in and join him.
"You have to see these fish, they are amazing." he said, taking the snorkel out of his mouth.
"I've got my coconut, I'll be there in a minute." I said chewing through a mouthful of coconut flesh.
"No seriously, you have to come now, they might not hang around for long."

I spent some more time nibbling on a few more spoonful's, in no hurry to go out and meet Hugh. I eventually Grabbed my snorkel gear and hastily put it on before I hopped and limped down the beach on the crunchy coral to the water and dived in. The refreshing water enveloped me. I had been oblivious to the heat of the sun, mesmerised by the coconut. I swam over to where Hugh was and he started pointing at a head of coral and dived under to show me the place to look. It was full of tiny little fish that glittered in the sunshine, they looked to be silver and reflected the shimmering of the sunlight through the water. I gave a thumbs up to Hugh under water and he pointed for me to keep looking at a busy school of fish circling the coral. Hugh started getting more insistent and pulled my arm so that I could see what he was gesturing at. Then I spotted it, glimmering in the light and flickering as the waves above distorted the beams of the sun's rays. A ring. With a diamond on it. I looked at Hugh and my eyes felt like they were going to pop out of my head. I could see him grinning even though he had the snorkel in his mouth. He grabbed the ring off the coral and together we came up to the surface. I just looked at him with wide eyes and a slack jaw, speechless. My mouth opened noiselessly like a fish trying to get air.

"This is for you." he said.
"But…how…what?" I asked awkwardly through the snorkel.
"This is for you. Will you marry me?"
I pulled my face mask up to my forehead and kept blinking in disbelief. "Um, of course. Yes!"

Time slowed down, I could not believe that this was happening; it was such a shock. I wrapped my legs around his waist while he still paddled in the water. He grabbed my left hand and put the ring on my ring finger. We kissed the most passionate kiss for what felt like an eternity. His face was cold from the water and his lips salty but it didn't matter. I threw my arms around his neck and we stayed embraced while Hugh struggled to keep us both above water as small waves slopped around our faces.

"Are you sure?" I asked.

"Of course I am sure."

"How did it get…hang on…did you put it on that coral?"

He looked at me with disbelief. "Did you think it was just here and I seized the moment or something?"

"Oh, I don't know. This is so cool… I'm glad I left my coconut."

"So am I. I didn't think you would come!"

"Well it was worth it!". We kissed again and continued to paddle around snorkelling for a bit holding one hand as we looked at the coral reef below. I couldn't wipe the smile off my face.

When we were closer to shore Hugh pulled over the dingy to more shallow water and we both hopped in sitting on opposite sides to keep it balance. Then he started up the outboard engine and steered us to where our boat was anchored. I was in shock at what has just happened. We were on the other side of the atoll so it was a long trip back and I enjoyed the wind in my face and looked back to see Hugh smiling and his jaw soften. I could see him visibly unwind and let go of the anxiety he must have been holding.

Once back on our boat, we grinned at each other.
"So you swam over to that bit of coral holding the ring and put it on?" I asked.
"Yeah, well I actually had it tied to a string and tied into my shorts pocket so that it wouldn't fall out while we were getting there. I haven't had this ring on board for a year and half to lose it now."
"You've had it for how long? What?" I asked. I couldn't hide my surprise. "Where did you get it? Where did you hide it so that I wouldn't find it?"
"I bought it in Darwin, just before we left for Indonesia. I felt that we had been through enough by then, you know, crossing the Gulf of Carpentaria. We were just about to launch into the unknown and you were still keen, even despite the sea sickness. I knew it then."
"Wow, I had no idea. Why did you do it here, there have been so many wonderful places?"
"We were on our way home. This is the last stretch, we will be in Australia in just a few weeks. We will be home. I wanted to show you that we were in it together when we got back, that it wasn't just about the boat and the trip, it is forever. That we were together despite the sailing trip. I knew you were thinking about who we would be together when we got back."

I leant over and kissed him. It struck me that it really had been worrying me that when all the excitement and wonder of the trip was over that I thought our life would be too boring for Hugh. That he would seek out more adventures to try and out-do this one. It would be a never-ending competition to always try and be more outgoing and see things and places differently, better than the time before. But by putting this ring on my finger, he wanted to make our life together the adventure.

"So where did you have the ring on the boat all this time?" I asked.

"I had it tucked in the electrical switchboard. Pushed down in the corner. Do you remember when Russell the rat was on board?"

"How could I forget?" I snorted.

"Well it turns out that Russell got in there and nibbled on the ring box, the little bastard seemed to have a taste for fine metals." Hugh went down into the cabin and produced the box with delicate teeth marks all around one side.

I laughed. "Oh my god! That rat. Oh Russell, he knew before I did about the ring. Lucky he didn't eat the thing!"

"That was why I wouldn't let you go in to the switch and see if there was damage, I couldn't have you pulling out the box in that filthy marina and ruining the moment for when I would ask." he paused as he smiled. "Then today I was so worried that when I put it on the coral that it would float off with the moving current or a fish would come by and swallow it up! Could you imagine? And you wouldn't bloody well get off the beach because you were eating your damn coconut!"

I laughed sheepishly. "But I did swim out to the coral where you were. It all worked out."

"Hmmm." he murmured.

"I would like to point out that you chose this location very strategically. I mean, there is only one other way off this island if not on this boat," I said as I tapped the seat, "and that is on the twice-yearly supply ship to Pohnpei, five long day's journey from here. What would have happened if I said 'no'?" I asked.

"You were never going to say 'no'. Were you?"

"Lucky you didn't ask me while I was feeling sea sick!" I said, leaning back into his arms. We both sat in silence slowly sipping on our rum drinks in the warm afternoon sun, reflecting on the day. I started thinking about returning to life back in Sydney and it felt like this changed everything, that it answered some questions and we would be doing it all together. Starting again together and deciding on our future together. It was a good feeling. No, actually, it was a great feeling.

CHAPTER SEVENTEEN

The Church

The sound of the singing erupted around us in the small concrete church. This one woman, small in stature, slightly stooped, about 70 with white wispy hair and an intense, loud voice, had the role of starting everyone off. It was as if her voice rang a bell; she was the instrument that would sound the starting note for the song. The room was silent, save her bold voice. After a few of her lead-in words the ladies in the congregation joined-in, in unison with her, they would pause and then the men would continue, it was a call and response song which culminated in the most spine chilling harmony from the entire congregation. Most of the village was there, maybe 100 people, children, teenagers, their parents and the elders too. All singing; all completely immersed. They poured out the words with passion. I could remember some of the songs from my childhood in church services, the same hymns with the same rhythm and melody, though they were singing in Kapinga and the only common word that I could pick up between the languages was 'Jesus'.

We were nearing the end of our stay on Kapingamarangi so Hugh and I had decided to attend the local church service, seeing as we were there on a Sunday. We were interested to see how engaged the community still were with Christianity. Summoned by the ringing of the enormous village bell we made our way to church for their weekly service. Darkness fell over the village soon after we arrived on shore and as the sun set we could hear the generator hum to life as it powered the single globe inside the church building. We entered and sat in the middle of the room on some uncomfortable wooden pews – a feature of churches worldwide it seemed. It took a while for the building to fill and no one would sit next to us until the Reverend invited them to; they were still quite shy around us. Reverend Yoster stood at the front of the church and began to welcome the congregation. But the service really opened with the singing, the loud bellowing of the one voice that started the group off. It was different to other church services as it was not a choir or group performing for the congregation, but the whole building, every person within it sang in glorious harmony together. No instruments, no music in the background, no hymn books or papers, just a whole room of passionate people singing together to songs that they knew by heart.

The sermon that the Reverend gave to the group was unfortunately for us, all in Kapinga, but we could pick up on the gist of it and the passion presented in the congregation's harmonic singing of hymns came to us as their storytelling and was a treat to listen to. The Reverend Yoster was kind enough to translate for us, and he invited us to speak to the congregation at the end of the service, where we thanked the islanders for their warm welcome of us to their home. They beamed with appreciation and it was good to be able to express our gratitude for them letting us visit here. At the end of the service we were invited to Pastor Rue's place for coffee with some of the congregation. His house was the palm tree hut with the raised palm log with woven leaf flooring that we had become used to seeing. We sat next to Rue's hut on some palm tree logs as the Reverend lit a fire to provide lighting for our gathering. I had brought along a banana cake that I'd made on board to include on the supper table, and Rue gave us a gift of a pumpkin which almost made my eyes pop. I was very excited to see fresh food! While he spoke English, he talked very little and mostly we sat in silence and watched the church group sit and chatter to each other.

Grateful for our time with the community and our pumpkin we retired back to the boat for the night.

The next day we visited Sakius again, eager to talk about the book that we had read. And we passed on to him some books about history that we had on the boat and hoped that he would like. But he was more interested in talking about current affairs.

"So there are lots of young people here, have they finished school?" asked Hugh.

"Yes, they have come back here. But many do not. They stay in the United States or Fiji and get jobs that you can't do here. I am very sad because I feel that there is a great loss of craftsmanship, like with the wooden canoes that are our tradition, for our fishing. But now the people just get fiberglass boats brought here and they don't know how to fix it if it breaks and that means we don't get fish. It's really sad and I feel like our cultural traditions of passing down skills is dying." replied Sakius.

"So the whole lifestyle here used to be completely self-sufficient, I mean, it's hard to rely on the supply ship, right?" said Hugh.

"Yes, even now it is two months late in arriving. And the ship is a new thing, there were never supply ships before the Japanese. The supply ships came so that they could build their bunkers and bring ammunition and food for their soldiers who were stuck here during the war. For some reason the Japanese thought this was a useful place to have an attacking base. They were wrong. The only thing that happened was the US bombed us here. It was very sad. This is what my mama told me anyway, I was not here. You can see the old watch towers and many of these concrete buildings were the houses of the Japanese senior military who lived here to rule over us and their soldiers." said Sakius.

"It's amazing to come from where we are from, to see that a whole society can survive on such a small island like this, grow their own food and build or make almost everything that they use from palm trees." said Hugh.

"We are a very smart people, all these skills have been passed down for hundreds of years from our ancestors. We have also survived through all these various rulers coming and going. But it is now we see the biggest threats to our lifestyle and our island. We have an internet dish here. You might have seen it at the primary school, but there is no connection because it costs too much, so no one has the internet. There is also only a computer in the school, but no one knows how to use it even if they were sat down in front of it. We have no mobile phones here. The Chief, he has a HF – long distance radio. He can speak with Pohnpei, but it is rarely used. We have no real electricity either. But these are not the threats. These are the things that keep us remote and protected from the outside world. I mean the kids, they see the outside world when they go to school in Pohnpei. They see television, they learn how to use computers and see the internet and watch things that happen in the United States, but they have to choose when they finish school, where to live, in the old world – here. Or in the new world – there. It is hard to see, but there is some good news, we have some kids that go to university and come back here as teachers, like Afu over there. Hey Afu, *hani, hani* - come here." he called to a young guy walking past.

Afu came over, he had been shaving copra "*Ora Na Sakius.*"

"Tell these people why you came back here, after you go to Hawaii for university?" Sakius asked.

"This is my home. I want more people to come back here too." Afu said.

"So you don't want television and the internet?" asked Hugh.

"Why would I give this up? Look at this, it is paradise. It is my home." Afu responded, as he waved his hand to the lagoon water beyond.

We couldn't argue with that. He walked off to sit back with his friends.

"But something we can't stop is climate change." said Sakius. "The University of Hawaii installed a small weather system on our pier. It is there to measure water height and sea temperature and other conditions."

"We saw that, but didn't know who was collecting the information." said Hugh.

"They installed it to try and study the rise in sea levels. We are slowly going under water. We have some salty water here in the island, the water table is getting higher and ruining our crops, we had to move some of our gardens." said Sakius.

He had made a solemn point. The sea level had only to rise half a metre or so before the ocean swell would overcome the island. Other reminders of the outside impacts on the atoll were around too, like on the incoming tide, we were saddened to see a line of plastic rubbish floating to shore. None of this waste was sourced from the atoll - as they did not buy bottled water or polystyrene boxes - but the rubbish had floated hundreds of miles on the ocean currents to mar these otherwise spotless beaches. The locals were left to clean up the waste and either reuse it, bury it or burn it. It was a sobering reminder of the outside world impacting life in such a remote place; its interconnectedness despite its isolation, the vast surrounding ocean dwarfing the atoll.

As we walked along the sand of the beach on our last day at the atoll and Hugh and I talked about our trip, about the adventure, and about how it had changed us. We spoke about how we were on our way home. It felt like an age since we had left Australia, but I really didn't know how much I had changed. We had had so many amazing experiences. We decided that we were both looking forward to being back in the familiar. We continued discussing what the experience meant to us and how it had impacted us.

"It's hard to describe, I feel like we are the same but not quite the same as the people that left Sydney. It isn't some sharp change in who we are, more another layer, the perspective we have gained I guess. That you can live a very enriched life without most of the things that we have in our Australian life, just think about the people here, on Kapingamarangi." I said.

Hugh rubbed his stubble as he thought more deeply. Then he turned and gazed out across the lapping water of the atoll, toward the horizon where the sky met the ocean. It was hard to see the difference between the sky and water because the richness in each of the blues blended to become one.

"I got an appreciation of that concept in those places I worked for the UN, those developing nations. That the important things in life really boil down to just a few things like freedom or empowerment, and connection – like to family or friends or the land. We get so caught up in having stuff in our lives and it is scary to see what that obsession with stuff is doing and the strain that this need for more things in putting on natural resources and the environment." said Hugh.

"I know, I just think back to all that rubbish we saw in the ocean in Indonesia and here, on the pristine beaches. If we didn't wrap everything in plastic half of that waste wouldn't exist. We are choking in our own obsession with having more things. We are killing the oceans." I said.

We continued walking and I kicked at some lumps of sand to send it spraying into the rising tide on our way to see the Chief.

We walked around the island one last time and said goodbye to the Chief and told him we would be leaving the following day. We thanked him for his generosity in letting us stay and bid him farewell with a handshake.

Hugh and I walked hand in hand down the concrete pier for one last time. It was sad for us to leave such a beautiful place, especially as it now had such a personal significance for us

CHAPTER EIGHTEEN

Another Seven Hundred Miles

It was an inky black moonless night, maybe 11pm, the wind was howling and the boat was being pounded by rain and waves. It didn't look like much on the weather forecast, but the predictions were rarely accurate in this remote part of the Pacific. It'd been like this for hours and had the potential to last another day. I looked over at Hugh. He had come up on deck because it was so noisy and uncomfortable down below. And he must have seen the exhaustion in my eyes because he made the decision to heave-to – to set the boat so that it was pointed into the wind, stopping it from moving forward - an age-old tool used by sailors to weather a storm. I would have been scared in weather like this a year ago. But spending more time at sea, sailing on my own at night and knowing our boat helped me find some calm while managing the heavy weather – it was becoming routine. We had sailed through so much adverse weather over the preceding months that calm seas seemed like a dream I had had once.

Hugh looked so weary, his eyelids were drooping, he had dark shadows under his eyes and he didn't want to make conversation. We had been at sea for six days and apart from our short magical stay in Kapingamarangi we were tallying up to have been almost a month at sea on this eastbound leg. The sailing over the previous week had been extremely tedious with winds that were light and unpredictable.

The light conditions had required us to constantly change the sail configuration and adjust our sailing plan to catch the fleeting winds. We would raise the spinnaker only to drop it again a few minutes later when a squall appeared and brought strong winds that would gust for a short while and then move off leaving us with choppy seas that were impossible to sail in. This went on and on, over and over, repeatedly sapping our energy. This leg had really worked our patience and we were tired and snapping at each other. We had crossed the equator heading south this time and the conditions were similar to the ones we had experienced

2000 miles ago in Asia, with the dead calms interspersed with fierce squalls around the equator. We held our equator crossing celebration, it was the second time we had crossed after doing it about a year before in Indonesia.

Sailing rituals have morphed to ensure cruisers partake in an equator crossing ceremony each time they cross. We gave shots of rum to ourselves before tossing one overboard for King Neptune – the King of the Sea, before jumping off the back of the boat into the water. Jumping off the boat in the middle of the ocean was daunting as it was against your instincts to leave the boat, especially when you are hundreds of miles from land. But we had dropped the sails so that the boat was barely moving and a refreshing dip broke the monotony. Equator crossing rituals of yesteryear involved dunking sailors off the side of boats and having them face 'the court' of King Neptune and his entourage before being declared a 'shell-back' – an experienced sailor who has crossed the equator. It was part of proving yourself as a sailor. Our ceremony was tamer but a necessary sailing ritual - one of many that are an integral part of the cruising experience.

Shortly after our equator crossing we were becalmed and we bobbed around, just rocking with the light swell as it rolled under the boat. The water reflected glass and as I squinted my eyes to look at the horizon, the ocean and the haze of the sky melted into one. It felt like we were alone, completely alone. Watching the sun as it moved through the sky was the only hint that time was passing. It was times like this that tested me; I was alone with my thoughts. The intensity of the feelings of isolation could be suffocating and I shudder to think of the many people who had suffered weeks and months of these conditions in times gone by with dwindling supplies to add stress to the situation. As someone who never sought out solitude, this was an unwelcome experience for me. We had been becalmed before for about three days, when we were crossing the South China Sea between Malaysia and Borneo, but that felt different because it was between two pieces of land. I had an undiminishing hope that we would eventually float towards our destination, I felt very protected there because they were well travelled waters full of boating traffic. But here, out here in what seemed like the wide open ocean it was a different feeling altogether. We hadn't seen any boats out here in the Pacific Ocean, it felt like just us and the sea. I would go through things in my mind, analyse the sail configuration a million times, look at the ropes and their condition over and over and over. There is so much time and no activity to fill it. It's hard to talk about how we passed the time, because it seemed like we did nothing. No talking, no movement. Nothing. For days. Just hoping for the weather to change.

There was a short period when a group of birds flocked to the boat. They were tiny little wrens and it seemed like they were just looking for somewhere to land and rest after flying at sea. We were 500 miles from land and these tiny little birds must have been flying for days and days. One morning as I did the dawn shift they descended on the boat, just one to start with, then another and another, eventually about ten of these tiny brown birds sought refuge on our boat. Sitting on the ropes, the cockpit cushions and eventually my finger. It was wonderful to see life. The little birds reaching about 10cm in height stood on their feet before they eventually rested their orange crested bellies on the cushions and closed their eyes. They were beautiful birds and they looked so calm. I wondered endlessly about where they had come from, where such tiny creatures would store the energy required for their long flying journey. I made up the conversation that the ring leader had with the other birds when trying to convince them to come on a flying mission of certain death over the open ocean. Then before we knew it, they were gone again, they were recharged and ready for their next leg. But the chance meeting had invigorated me, reminded me that we would end our time at sea and we would make it to land. It was a welcome break in the seeming unending monotony of the ocean passage.

Not long after our brief visit from the little birds the wind came. Hugh and I were relieved and the fluky winds, hot humid calms and squally storms of the equator were almost behind us as we slowly made our way south towards the

Solomon Islands and hopefully into some favourable trade winds. Our joy at welcoming the return of the wind was short lived as we were soon thrust into the storm.

We worked through the motions of 'heaving-to' barely talking. Hugh turned the boat into the wind while I groaned and struggled to furl in the heavy jib sail which was hard to do as the conditions had worsened and the wind had picked up to over 35 knots. We had practised this manoeuvre months before in the Philippines and read about the technique over and over to make sure that we both knew what to do in case we had to do it in an emergency. I unfurled the smaller staysail which helped to balance the boat while it was pointed into the wind and Hugh tied off the helm so that the boat pointed correctly. The intent of the manoeuvre was to stop us moving forward and sit in line with the wind as the storm passed over instead of struggling to sail with it.

Almost instantly, the noise around us quietened and everything felt calmer, the change in the boat motion was astonishing. The boom was not banging and the boat just comfortably rolled over the waves like a cork floating in water. While the conditions had not changed, the way that we experienced them had. It really made for a comfortable way to sit out a storm rather than constantly fighting against it and straining the boat in such strong conditions. We hadn't made the change earlier because we were hoping the conditions would improve and we could keep moving forward, but as the storm persisted we decided we should rest instead. After we changed the sails, Hugh told me to go to bed and get some sleep, he would rest in the cockpit and keep an eye on things.

I was grateful to be sent to bed as I couldn't get enough sleep. I struggled with the three-hour sleeping rotation that we did on passage - I really treasure my sleep. Waking up at 10pm for my three-hour shift and again at 4am was trying my patience. I would sleep during the day for a couple of hours to try and catch up, but after a week I was grumpy, lethargic and sick of being on the boat.

Hugh managed a bit better usually, but this trip had taken its toll on him too and he was bored and tired. We both needed a break from the monotony of sailing. We each had been listening to audio books but most of our other distractions had gone. Two of our laptops got saturated when water came into the cabin and damaged them on the passage from Palau to Kapingamarangi, so that killed our movie collection and computer games. We were also out of range of the AM radio stations that we could pick up on the HF radio. We had finished all of the books on the boat and had run out of fresh food so there was no reading or cooking to do. After so long at sea together we certainly had nothing to talk about. We would make a cordial drink for each other sometimes to try and punctuate the day, but all in all, it was tedious. To break up the day we used the HF radio to send and receive emails. It worked by connecting a laptop to a modem which connected to the HF radio. The modem was similar to the dial-up internet that we used in our houses in the 1990s; it was glacially slow and depending on the weather and atmospheric interference we often didn't get a signal at all. The connection was especially poor where we were in the Pacific Ocean and far from the receivers in Australia and Asia. So maybe we would get the connection every two or three days. Hugh's sister would send us daily quotes, random lines from her favourite books. That day it was a quote from Wodehouse and it read "He was standing on his left leg. With a sudden change of policy, he now shifted and stood on his right." I had a chuckle and took our tiny backup laptop to Hugh so that he could read it. A small grin spread across his face. It was nice to have those breaks in the day and to feel like we were not alone out here.

At about 5am Hugh woke me up to help him change the sails, the storm had passed and the wind had calmed down and had moved to be on the beam, just the right angle to get us closer to the Solomon Islands. So I took over the sailing while he went down below to get some rest. The sky started to change from black to grey with some light yellow glimmers appearing on the horizon. In the cold light of the breaking day I could make out some movement near the bow of the boat, so I went up to see a huge pod of dolphins diving and playing in the bow wave. It was very special, I loved seeing the dolphins and we hadn't seen any for a while so it lifted my spirits and I started to get excited about our arrival in the Solomons. It looked like we would arrive later that day in the anchorage Hugh had picked.

Later that morning after he had a bit of a sleep Hugh joined me in the cockpit. We started talking about our feelings on leaving home, these kinds of conversations were more frequent since we were coming to the end of the journey – the return to Australia.

"What have you learnt from this trip?" asked Hugh.

I took a moment and looked off the side of the boat. "I have learnt that life is wonderful. You have to grab it by both hands to see what is out there. Fear about the future and uncertainty should be thrown aside if you are ever to experience what is out here. Leaving Sydney was hard, we had to give up our comforts, jobs and securities to go out on a boat." I said.

"That was hard. And we were praised and criticised for that, some people thought it was a great idea while others, like your dad were worried for you, that life would pass you by if you didn't stay on the known track of life, that you would miss out on something." said Hugh.

"I know. I suppose for him it is hard to conceive of a life different to that which you have lived and seen all those around you live. I guess it is about your character and whether you can cope with change and have the courage to say when you made a mistake. This whole thing could have ended five minutes after we left Sydney heads the way I was feeling when I was so seasick. So to come back could have been that defining moment of admitting defeat." I said.

"I don't know what is more scary! Leaving the lives we had established or having to come back not accomplishing anything." said Hugh.

"Once you get over the fear of change and committing to the unknown, everything else is easy I think."

"What do you mean the 'unknown'?"

"Well we didn't know what was out here, whether I would cope with seasickness, whether the boat would be okay, we also didn't know where we were going, and we didn't know how we would go as a couple on a boat, there was so much unknown."

"Well I am glad that we got that last one sorted out, two people in a confined space is a test of character!" said Hugh, grinning.

We sat back and enjoyed the slow rocking motion of the boat as the wind comfortably pushed the boat along in the calm protected waters of the Solomon Islands chain. The sound of the boat carving through the water made a soft whooshing sound interspersed with the rare splashing sound of a low wave hitting the hull and breaking.

In the early afternoon we could see the mountainous landscape of Vella Lavella Island as we drew nearer. The water had changed colour to a lighter blue as the it became shallower and I could see in the distance the water breaking over the reef that encircled the land. Butterflies rose in my stomach as we started to prepare for our entry. We had spoken to some other cruisers months before in Malaysia who had given us some vague waypoints for entering the cove here, but there were no markers on the reef, we just had to try and spot the entry with our eyes. Hugh had downloaded a google earth map and overlaid a sailing map on top, a very rudimentary mapping method. We had a nerve-wracking reef entry, again! So I stood up on the bow and signalled to Hugh who was sitting in the cockpit steering the boat away from where underwater obstacles were. They seemed to be everywhere, I breathed in deeply as we crossed the bar as I hoped we would make it. There was just enough water depth for us to make it over the coral heads that marked the shallow bar entry and we emerged into a small circular harbour.

As we dropped anchor on the edge of the mangrove-ringed cove and turned the boat engine off, my ears rang with the sudden quietness and it took a while to adjust to the tranquil place we were in. The boat was stationary and not making a noise, the water was flat with barely a ripple marking the crystal clear surface and the silence was only interjected with a sudden myriad of bird calls and the rustle of dense green palm trees that ringed the shore. It was not long until nightfall and forks of yellow lightning illuminated the purple and black sky as it flashed over the mountains in the distance.

We had just completed a 700 mile passage from Kapingamarangi Atoll and it had taken a painstaking seven days. This was a milestone. It marked the end of our Pacific Ocean crossing from Palau to the Solomons, we were edging ever closer to home.

CHAPTER NINETEEN

The Trade Economy

Our first few days of convalescence in Vella Lavella harbour were blissful. The word 'harbour' is generous by western terms as there was not a dock, pier, mooring or boat in sight. Its definition as a harbour comes from the historical use of the word as a natural harbour, a place to hide a boat from weather or contrary sea conditions. While occasionally we spotted some locals fishing from hand paddled canoes along the river banks, we kept to ourselves and relaxed listening to a myriad of unfamiliar bird calls, watching crocodiles slink below the water's surface where the water mingled with mud and the roots of the mangroves, and the wide array of sea life that darted about the coral suffused bay. At one end of the cove a mangrove forest ringed the crystal clear waters that exposed the coral seascape below. This was a completely unique experience for us. The colours here were in stark contrast to mangroves in Asia and Australia because the mangrove edge was usually the meeting point of salt and fresh water creating a murky water colour. The coral diversity of the harbour was something to behold, with fan structures and table tops strewn amongst large coral bommies. The fish life included large angel fish, anemones and countless other iridescent fish darting from place to place. The parrot fish looked relaxed while munching on coral - so loud you could hear them crunching while sitting on the boat admiring them from above.

The second day after we arrived, a local man stopped by to ask us if we had seen some students who had gone out fishing in canoes. He was a skinny man with black disheveled hair and his skin was so dark it was almost black; much darker than we had seen with other local people like in Palau or at Kapingamarangi. He grinned and showed us his broken red stained teeth from the betelnut that he chewed. He introduced himself as Reggie and was very interested in our boat, so we invited him aboard as rain started to fall lightly around us.
"Come in out of the rain." Hugh said as he helped him tie his boat to ours and step aboard. "So what do you do Reggie?" I asked.

"I teach at Seventh Day Adventist School, I help with English." said Reggie in his heavy islander accent.

"Your English is very good, where did you learn it?" I asked.

"My parents were missionaries and English teachers, they make sure we spoke it." said Reggie.

"Do many people speak English here?" I asked.

"Some, but mostly pijin or tribal language. The British tried to make everyone speak English but not everyone go to school, so is more pijin." said Reggie.

"We read about the history here, that the British made it one of their colonies in 1900 and called it the British Solomon Islands." I said.

"Yes, but that was after the Spanish, they came here first. The British used the people and the land here to have plantations, to grow copra and rubber. But that stop in World War Two when Japanese come and took land and plantations. We get destroyed by war. The Americans come and brought tha cargo ships and tanks. For first time food and all tha supplies we could ever have wanted come on those big ships. We used to grow our own food and we would live off land, then all these things just arrive by boat and we forgot how to survive. The Americans even made capital city just for themselves, called Honiara, and they built a huge airforce base. But this became broken after the war bikos the Americans left, took with them their big ships and food no longer arrived. Our people starved, we had war with each other. The changes from the Americans didn't just undo after they left, our people were helpless to go back to their old lives." said Reggie.

"We have seen that where we have been in the Pacific. The war completely changed life on these islands and now the people are dependent on food and aid being brought in from other countries." said Hugh.

I went down below and fixed Reggie a drink of water and some nuts for a snack. He gratefully accepted and gobbled up the food and I wondered if he got much to eat.

"So do you grow your food at the school?" I asked.

"Yes, fruit and vegetables. We also have some chickens. But sometimes we go get supplies like rice or flour. We have to go to Gizo for that, the big town. I go on a banana boat, you know, a small fiberglass boat with an engine. It is a long two and a half hour trip. It's over that way," he gestured with his hand, "but I don't go too much, is long way and sometimes we don't have petrol." said Reggie.

"So is it safe here now? There was some war here in Honiara, different tribes fighting?" I asked.

"Is better now, but Honiara is dangerous place. When tha British and Americans came here to build airforce they imported labour from all over the Solomon Islands. They mixed tha local people with those from other islands. It was very bad. Before the war people didn't go outside their tribe except to find a bride or to trade. There has been an ongoing problem in Honiara with local and non-local people. But they have lived in Honiara for over 50 years now and they think they should be locals too. So the fighting was about land ownership. There was a political coup, the country order disappear, food and supplies were cut off from import and it was very bad. Many people died. It went on for more three years until the Australians' sent in peace-keeping force to try and calm things down, restore trade." said Reggie.

"Are there still some bad places?" asked Hugh.

"Some, but Gizo and around here is fine. You just have to watch people drinking alcohol, alcohol is very bad. People get violent, but not so many people drink alcohol, many people are religious." said Reggie.

"So you are Seventh Day Adventist?" I asked.

"Yes, many people here are, missionaries came here in 1800s and brought religion to local villagers. My parents were missionaries and spent a lot of time in Papua New Guinea teaching tha people there." said Reggie.

The rain had cleared and Reggie said it was getting late and that he needed to get back to the village. He thanked us for the rest from the rain and slowly putted away in his small boat and disappeared around the corner of the cove out of sight. Once again we felt completely alone. There were obviously people that lived near here, but they were tucked away in the jungle away from sight from the water. We wanted to go and visit Reggie and his school but it was a bit of a dangerous trip in our dingy without knowing the exact way over the reef.

We were grateful for the chance meeting and to hear about the Solomon Islands from a local.

The next day we took the boat to Gizo. It wasn't a long trip, but there were periods of heavy rain and we ended up motoring most of the way as the wind was changing a lot. The entry was marked as bigger ships sometimes went there, but it was still challenging as we were not confident with the markers. I was up on the bow again, with my heart racing as we maneuvered through the reef entry to the town. The entry was easy compared to the ones we had done recently. It seemed that the waterway was dredged and cleared to make sure that it was still able to cope with the commercial shipping boats. It was late afternoon by the time we found a spot to drop anchor, just to the north of the town. The reef circling the island protected it from swell so the water was calm and flat. We prepared to go ashore and get some dinner, we had both been looking forward to a meal off the boat on our long days at sea.

We had slowly made our way past town to the place where we anchored. We saw a large concrete jetty – where the larger cargo boats would dock, and a row of tiny single story timber shacks with red tin rooves that lined the foreshore. It was the back of the shacks that we could see, they were facing the town, not the water.

We launched the dingy from our boat and made our way to shore. There was a restaurant just near where we were anchored that had a small jetty coming out from it. It was obviously a place that welcomed us yachties and you could use their jetty if you bought some of their food or drink. I gingerly stepped out of the dingy and felt a surge of energy, something that came to me when I walked on solid ground after so much time on a moving boat. We had both been imagining what the Solomons would be like and what Gizo - their second biggest town would look and feel like. I was filled with excitement and intrigue. We told the barman that we were just going for a walk and we would be back for dinner soon and we emerged from the bar to a dusty street lined with small houses or shacks made from sheets of timber with corrugated iron sheet roofing. The buildings were meagre and I found it hard to believe that they would protect the people inside from any bad weather. The town reminded me of Thursday Island, that tiny island at the north of Australia, a short skip between the Australian mainland and Papua New Guinea, it had the same shack type buildings, same red dirt roads and the same small type of beat up old cars from the 1990s.

We were at one end of the town, it was quiet with a few people walking along the sides of the street, but there was not much noise. As we walked closer to the centre of town we spotted the customs building, where we would have to go the next day when they were open to make our visit official and have our paperwork stamped. There were a number of small shops with roller shutter doors opening out to the street and they were selling takeaway fish and chips wrapped in paper but I saved myself for the dinner we were going to have at the bar.

At the centre of town was the market place. But because it was the evening nothing was for sale, except some guys selling betelnut which was a mix of the red nut with some lime powder and a tiny amount of tobacco. The people here rolled it into a ball and chewed it sometimes for hours and it was touted to give a small high like smoking cigarettes. The problem was that the red pigment of the nut stained their mouth and the lime powder rotted their teeth and so their smile was a little off-putting, like there was blood in their toothless mouths. They would also spit a red ball on the ground periodically while chewing, and it stained the street and the walls of buildings. Betelnut was very popular in the Pacific and variations of it existed throughout Asia as well.

We found ourselves at the end of the main street as it was very short, but there were a couple of streets coming off it leading to a few houses which were a combination of the Queenslander timber houses on stilts to let a cooling breeze through and some more palm tree type houses with palm leafed roofing – a midway design from the houses we had seen in Kapingamarangi and the Queenslander houses with the open ground floor. It turned out that there was not a whole lot to see of the town. But it was still so much more interesting than sitting on the boat.

By this time our hunger had set in and we went back to the bar for dinner. We looked at the menu, filled with delicious seafood dishes and Hugh immediately decided to have a crayfish, they were abundant around here and the Seventh Day Adventists didn't eat them as they believed it was not right to eat shellfish. In the end we both got one and washed it down with a cold local SolBrew beer. It was one of the most delicious meals I had ever had and I sat back and rested into the chair with my shoulders down and a warm feeling of relaxation came over me. It was so nice to be in a comfortable port again and to have some fresh and different food cooked for us.

The next day we checked in with the customs office and again there were many sheets of paper to fill out and questions to answer. The official was very polite and like those we had met in Indonesia and Asia, he was wearing a crisp white ironed shirt and pressed pants. He didn't ask us many questions. I don't think he really cared for small talk or conversation with us and efficiently processed our papers to send us on our way.

While we were still walking in town we picked up some supplies at the fresh market, some *kabis* or green vegetables, tomatoes, cucumber, bananas, eggplant and eggs, just enough for a day or two. We had become used to buying these items in the islands, these were the foods that were easy to grow in the weather and soil conditions. The food offerings were slim and the locals said that it was not the usual *maket* – or market day, so we had the *lelebet* – small bits from the previous days. We also bought a treat of some imported Australian cheese from the small store before getting two servings of fried fish and sweet potato chips wrapped in paper from a small takeaway shack; a delicious lunch.

We had completed our formalities and picked up some supplies, so we left Gizo and continued our travel south through the Solomon Islands chain. We were looking for a small cove to stop in and found one on the map that was a short day trip from Gizo which looked like it would be well protected from the sea swell of the main passage, it was called Ringgi Cove. We did not really know what to expect here, and after dropping anchor inside the bay which was ringed by dense jungle we could see two small family houses made from palm tree trunks and palm leaves close to the water's edge. Shortly after we arrived we were visited by some young local girls who had paddled up in a small hand carved canoe that was barely above the waterline. There were three girls in the canoe with the eldest seemingly not more than eight years of age who gave us a bunch of flowers, and another girl, like her little sister sitting crouched behind her shyly and holding another of their siblings, that looked no more than four years old. They didn't speak English and just handed us the flowers and giggled. They were about to paddle away, but we stopped them and handed some exercise books and colour pencils down to their small canoe. Their eyes lit up and they quickly paddled away back to the small houses that sat on the shore. The following day we were visited by some more canoe going locals and we traded sugar, flour, tea, milk powder, soap and kids clothes for an absolute feast of fresh vegetables.

"Look at all this food". I exclaimed to Hugh, my eyes beaming.

"I wonder if they have this much to spare." he said.

"I hope that what we gave them was a good trade." I said.

"Yeah, it's hard to know what's a fair amount of other things to swap for their own homegrown produce." said Hugh.

We decided to take our dingy in to shore to speak to one of the families. Only the father could speak a little English.

"Do you live on your own here?" asked Hugh.

"Yes, this *wantok*, my *mami* and *pikinini*." the man responded, he was gesturing to his wife, mother and children of which there were six, including the three girls who had paddled out to visit us with flowers the day before. They were sitting on the dirt ground which was pounded hard from use and the women were preparing some fresh vegetables for a meal. The flattened ground was below an upper level of palm tree and leaf construction forming a roof which looked like where they slept when it was raining. I could see cooking utensils, pots and pans next to some palm leaf woven mats that some of the children were sitting on. The girls were wearing ragged dresses with some small holes or frayed edges while the boys and their father wore faded shorts and no t-shirt. The women wore big dresses that were also well worn with faint floral patterns. They all walked around with no shoes. Some of the boys were frolicking in the shallow water that was next to the house, pretending to catch small fish with their hands while their father spoke with us.

"I work for logging company." he said as he pointed over to the far end of the cove and we could see a dirt road leading up to the ridge. "This close to work so we live here, but work only some of time, now is off time."

"Thank you for letting us stay here. It is a beautiful place." said Hugh.

The woman smiled. She was happy for some of the trade and for us to play with her children for a little while. We towed the kids around with our dingy by a rope tied to their canoe and they laughed and enjoyed the fun of having visitors in the cove, yelling *tanggio tanggio* – thank you - to us as we waved goodbye.

We had heard from some other cruisers about the World War Two relics in the area. There was a Japanese gun emplacement the next cove along, so the next day we set out in our dingy to travel around and go for a walk in the jungle. When we arrived some local boys took us through the thick jungle to see the abandoned weapons. We were macheted our way through the dense jungle growth, clambering over fallen trees, slipping and sliding through the muddy jungle floor to see these enormous gun emplacements. The effort the soldiers had to go through to bring the guns was astounding. The guns were dug into the ground and would require the gunner to sit in a hole, a mud pit, swatting mozzies and trying to spot aircraft overhead while heavy monsoonal rains fell on them, it must have been a grim situation.

After a short three-day stay in Ringgi, we continued the short half-day sail to the grimy town of Noro, famous for its fish canning factory and also the main port for all of the Solomons for international shipping. We intended to only be here for a day so we could do the formalities of checking out before heading south. The day was miserable, it was humid with little breeze and it was raining. It meant that visibility below the water was terrible as the glare from the overcast light gleamed off the surface of the water and we could not see the obstacles below. We ended up having to anchor two miles further down the waterway where we were out of the way of the massive coral shelf that the town seemed to be perched on.

After anchoring, Hugh took the dingy to town to do the checking out procedure and I stayed to watch the boat. We were planning to leave the Solomons in the coming days. While Hugh was out it started to rain, so I put our buckets out and opened the water tanks to collect the rainwater. It was only while I was out in the rain that I could see these shimmering movements on the surface of the water all around the boat and as I looked closer I could just see a fin, no two fins slightly skimming the surface before dipping down and away to resurface a few metres away. It was only after staring at this for some time that I realised that it was manta rays coming close to the water's surface to scoop up their dinner – plankton that must have been massing in the water below.

I couldn't take my eyes off these amazing creatures, we had seen some up close in Palau on a diving trip but the water was murky at the time. But here I could see them with amazing clarity, and I watched them for about an hour gliding around the boat, and as they turned they would delicately flick the edge of their wing at the surface before they dived to scoop up their micro-prey. While this was still continuing, Hugh emerged on the horizon zooming toward the boat in the dingy, he had had a successful trip with the authorities. Turns out I was mesmerised for about two hours watching the rays.

"You won't believe what is going on here," I said to Hugh. "Quick, put on your snorkel and flippers, we have to jump in the water." he followed my lead as I dug through out lazarette locker to find our gear, and we dived into the cool water. I swam over to where the manta rays were and Hugh followed me, I looked under the water to see his reaction when he saw what was going on, his eyes wide and even more magnified in the snorkel mask.

We made sure to keep out of the manta rays' path and just watched them as they continuously and systematically made turns to scoop up the plankton, as if they had a grid that they had to cover before they could finish their shift. Once we were in the water we could clearly see the plankton as it was a hazy green cloud that filled the water. This was such a rare experience as there are so few places where manta rays inhabit and we were so lucky to see them like this, it felt so intimate. It reminded us of one of the reasons why we would be on a trip like this – to see rarely seen animals in their natural habitat.

One of our last encounters in the Solomons was with another local man – Maru, a carver. Parts of the Solomons are famous for carvings, often bowls, utensils and small statues of the native wildlife and sea life that the culture relies on for survival. Maru came up to us in his small fiberglass boat and we invited him aboard. He didn't speak much English, but told us that he came from the islands north of Gizo where stone carving was the tradition.
"You want carvings?" he asked.

"Yes, what have you got?" Hugh asked.

Maru opened up his hessian sack to reveal some stone carvings in dark grey mottled colours, small warriors with spears and also some fish and turtle carvings.

"The carvings are very good." said Hugh.

"These ones very special." Maru said turning the small warriors in his hand showing us the smooth faces of the stone. "We make by taking stones from bottom of waterfall, only the ones with colours. We use old nail and strong stone to carve. We use water too, it work the stone."

Hugh took the warriors and looked intently at the intricacy of the carving. "It is very detailed."

"It takes long time." Maru said. He could tell that Hugh was hooked on the warriors.

"So what do you want for these?" Hugh asked as he pointed to the warriors and the turtle.

"My wife, she told me not to come home today if I do not get a phone." said Maru with a smile, he knew it was an outside chance.

We laughed, "You are not to come home?" I said. "What if you do not get a phone?"

"She was joking, well not really, she does want a phone." said Maru.

I could see Hugh thinking as he had a moment of realisation. "Oh, we have one. An old Nokia, it works and we have a charger." Hugh said.

I went down to the cabin below and riffled through some drawers to find the phone and the charging cable. The phone still turned on and Maru's eyes lit up.

"My wife, she will be very happy." he said and he bounced lightly on the cockpit seat.

Hugh and Maru shook hands. With a grin on his face, Maru stepped back into his boat and we watched him zoom off in the distance. Getting things in this country was so difficult we were learning, because the small villages were so far from the main trading ports, people rarely travelled there and had very little money with which to buy things anyway. The people lived a mostly self-sufficient and trading lifestyle and anything that they could not grow was a luxury.

As I carefully wrapped and put the carvings in the drawer of our cabin, I reflected on the way that trading was a core part of how people got the things they needed here, it felt good to be part of that system. So few people use money here, mostly it is trading by valuing what you have versus what you are trying to get from someone, a vastly different experience to shopping at home. It was Maru's lucky day that he ended up with a prized phone!

CHAPTER TWENTY

Coming Home

The whole time that we spent in the Solomons we had in the back of our minds that we were going home; that our big sailing trip was drawing to a close. I was filled with feelings of anticipation, wonder and excitement. It was hard to really envisage what returning would be like, what life for us would be like and how we would choose to live after this adventure. While we were still on the boat, I couldn't quite comprehend how the trip had changed us.

But first we had to make the last open ocean sailing leg from the Solomon Islands to Cairns on Australia's northeastern seaboard, across the Coral Sea. We had one false start; as we had prepared to leave one morning a weather report came in showing high winds and bad sea conditions, so Hugh decided that we should stay sheltered for a couple of more days. It was quite a deflating experience being all hyped up ready to start a passage and pulling the pin at the last minute, but it wasn't worth the risk to go if we felt a tinge of uncertainty. We stayed put and continued to dwell on what the last big sailing leg had in store for us.

Thankfully we were able to leave the Solomons on our second attempt. It had only been a short two-week stay in the island nation and it was such a beautiful place with wonderful people and we hoped to return one day. Once again as we set off, we were challenged by the weather and were faced with unreliable wind and hot dank weather that made for trying sailing conditions. However because we were refreshed from our time on land we were still in good spirits as we furled in the sails and reset them time after time as the winds shifted. These conditions lasted for about three days but as we pushed further south we hit the trade winds. Finally, with the sails full and the boat sailing at a comfortable pace, we were able to set the course and let our auto-pilot do the work. We were on the milk run back to Australia. The improved conditions continued to lift our mood and we spent time talking about what it was going to be like going back home.

"What has travelling by boat given you?" I asked.
"Well it forces you to slow down. Everything takes so much longer. I love the anticipation of arrival as you slowly draw closer to your destination. I love the feeling of connection to the past, to those explorers and navigators of yesteryear. Oh, and the natural feeling of the movement, the sailing motion, I find it very comforting, relaxing." said Hugh.
"Ugh, well, at least you like the motion, most of the time that motion makes me sick. But about arriving somewhere, sometimes it feels like we will never reach our destination because the wind stops or something." I said.
"Yeah, so patience is the other thing that sailing really tests you on. Whether you are a patient person or not, sailing like this forces you to become so. I noticed that your patience has improved" said Hugh with a smile.
"I know, I am not a patient person and that was one of the things that I really struggled with. I still would not describe myself as a patient person, but you have to submit to the weather and accept that you just have to wait longer. Like our failed departure from the Solomons just a few days ago. It is really deflating to be prepared to leave and then have to sit and wait it out. All that anticipation and build up to a departure leaves you with a feeling of disappointment when you don't leave."

"But it is better right? To wait rather than risk it." said Hugh.

"I'd say that is why we made it this far without too many dramas. Thankfully you're more patient that I am." I said. We reached across the cockpit to hold hands. I knew that without Hugh's sensible attitude to weather and sail planning we would have gone through rougher conditions that tested us and the boat and made for some bad outcomes.

As I felt the refreshing breeze on my arms, I knew that our arrival home would be the start of us planning our future together and it was going to be the beginning of an exciting new chapter in our lives. We sat back and soaked up the view, the endless blue that stretched to the horizon, no other boats, no land. Just us and the sea.

Later that night it was the total lunar eclipse where the moon would pass behind the earth's shadow. We had the perfect viewing for it, hundreds of miles from land and light and no obstacles like buildings. The day was cloudy and we just had to hope that the clouds would part for us to see the rare occurrence as it was to be fully visible in the northern Pacific. The boat was sailing along beautifully, the sails were set and I looked hopefully for vision of the moon.

The hours ticked by and the dense cloud covered my view of the sky beyond, but at around 11pm as the moon was high in the sky the clouds parted and I could see the moon and watch as it slowly changed colour to an eerie red. I tried to take a photo of it, but it was impossible to get a decent shot with the movement of the boat and the slowness of the camera shutter speed. So I sat back and stared as the moon made its track and changed colours from a mottled white to a brown to a reddish colour before returning to white again. Over the course of about an hour the moon had completed one of its rare but routine events. Being able to stare at the sky with nothing else to do was one of those special parts of the sailing experience.

It was on our ninth day at sea and we made our entry through the Great Barrier Reef just east of Cairns. We didn't want to be too complacent, but the passage was very well marked and it was easy to pass through. The navigation markers were the first sign that we were back in Australia. Then we heard noise on the radio with other boat chatter and we began seeing the myriad of navigation channel markers for the waterway leading to Cairns. This was a stark contrast to where we had recently been where we just had to judge the entry to the sailing channels by visually spotting and relying on the limited information we had from other people.

Cairns is obvious to see from afar due to the mountainous ranges that come close to the lands edge and dominate the landscape. The green tree covered hills were hazy with a light veil of salty sea mist locked in by the humid air. The sea water started to change colour as we progressed through the channel, as the muddy water from the inland waterways and mangroves was mixing with the clear blue ocean water.

We could hear the hum of civilization, with planes flying overhead and landing at the airport nearby and the engines of motorboats in the distance zipping through the channel. The sights and sounds of our homecoming dominated our senses as we drew nearer to shore, it almost felt like we were being propelled into the present from some distant past where none of these machines existed.

As with all the countries we had arrived in, we had formal checking-in procedures to adhere to. Being Australian and arriving into Australia was no different. We had to provide advance notice of our arrival, then tie up to the dock at the marina and have customs, quarantine and immigration come and check us in. This included the officers searching the boat and asking questions about where we had been, if we had contracted any illnesses and whether we were carrying any guns.
"So do you have any snakes or other animals on the boat?" asked the officer with much sincerity.

I laughed "what? No. I couldn't imagine anything worse than trying to live on a boat with a snake after the conditions we have been sailing in." I said.

The customs official didn't think that was funny but if only they had known how rough the first few days of the passage were, they would understand the sentiment of being trapped onboard with a seasick and angry snake. After customs we had quarantine, a bloke called Peter came aboard and we went through the items on his checklist. He took the scraps of fresh garlic we had left and inspected the small amounts of other food on board and saw no dramas with the canned food we still had. There was barely any fresh food left as we had eaten it over the last few days on passage. Then he spent the next 40 minutes pouring over the timber on the boat; he was looking for evidence of termites and other wood-borne infestations. He was also inquisitive about whether we had had any swarms of bees attack the boat, apparently a relevant risk in the Solomons; thankfully we had not. We got the tick of approval to enter.

All the procedural checking-in was routine and the officials were friendly enough. They were interested to hear about the story of our trip, but equally keen to get on with their other work tasks for the day.

Our next matter of business was indulging in some food cooked by someone else, a decidedly fantastic thing to do after spending so much time cooking for ourselves from a limited set of ingredients. So we slowly ambled down the main street and went to a restaurant to have a big fat juicy steak and tall cold beer. Hugh and I had been talking for days about what we would have as our first meal and steak was number one on the list. It had been such a long time. We had a steak in Thailand a year earlier that was imported from France, but that was the last time that we had had some delectable beef. And the beer was deliciously cold and refreshing, it really hit the spot. While we had the fridge on the boat, it had trouble keeping things cold in the heat of the tropics and most of the time our drinks were cool but not cold, so to have a drink with condensation streaming down the sides of the glass was a remarkable experience.

That night we went to stay with my sister Amie and her family. When I saw Amie her eyes were shiny and we hugged for what felt like an age, we were so happy to see each other. This is what I had missed while we were away: family, friends and the familiar. While being in new places and seeing new things is truly rewarding, I really craved the small things about the friendships and relationships that we had left. My four year old niece and two year old nephew ran to my knees and hugged me around my legs. They were such an affectionate pair and had grown up so much in the almost year and a half since we had seen them last in Cairns on our northbound leg. They were keen to show us their toys, so we were dragged away before any questions could be asked about the trip. Over the coming days we were immersed in their family life while we did some repairs to the boat and prepared it for the sail south. One night we sat down to dinner with Amie and her husband Steve, the kids were in bed and we had some time to talk together.

"So what was it like, living on a boat?" asked Amie.

"It's kind of like camping, you become quite self-sufficient, you pack as much food as you think you need and you make do a lot of the time, and you are completely exposed to the weather, it dominates your life." I said.

"It seems so surreal, to live out there on the water." said Amie.

"It didn't come easily to me," I said looking over at Hugh "but this guy, he loves it and is comfortable doing it, his confidence is contagious."

"Was it scary?" asked Amie.

"There were some moments. I guess I chose not to analyse things too much, I mean it is mostly out of our control, the weather and the things around us. The only thing you control are your decisions. We were very conservative, we chose not to sail in heavy conditions or go to some places because there were some risks about safety." I said.

"I still think that it is amazing, that you did this." said Amie.

"It was just an experience, we were just out there to see the world, and see it in a different way. We didn't do anything special. I feel like we were kind of closer to the local people. We did things that they did like buy food from the markets and buy supplies from the same hardware store and made do with what we could find, like they do. The difference was that we had many more comforts on the boat than they did in their homes, I mean we had electricity from the solar panels and the engine. We kind of lived like the people in some ways, but not all." I said.

"I just can't imagine it." said Amie.

"It's different." I said. We ruminated on that while we finished our dinner and packed away our plates before heading for bed.

The weather turned out to not be favourable for making-way south, so we ended up spending more time in Cairns than we had planned. But it was a fun time to spend slowly getting back into the Australian way of life and seeing how things had changed since we had been away. We had a new and very conservative Prime Minister and there had been changes to some policies but very little had changed in a visible way. Being in Cairns was good for us as it is a pretty quiet town and far from the big cities, a slow way for us to reintegrate into society.

There were three differences that struck me coming back, the first was talking. We had become used to not talking much, especially to each other as we didn't have much to say and if we were talking to locals, because they often spoke limited English, the conversations were quite short. I found I got very tired from having conversations and had to get used to talking at length again. I had to dig deep for my extended vocabulary which I had hardly used for most of the trip. I would tire easily from walking; I was not used to walking very far after so much time stuck on the boat and I so struggled to walk around Cairns for very long. The other obvious thing we noticed was going shopping for food or anything really – there was so much choice. The supermarkets were full of colour and noise, it was quite overwhelming as we had spent time in small stores or the fresh markets with very limited options.

We took our time trying to get used to everything here but we also went and hid on the boat if we needed some time away from it all. It was hard to change between the long periods of time we had spent in solitude to the civilisation here and getting used to the pace of things.

After two weeks the weather conditions improved so we started our trip south down the east coast back to Sydney, we hoped to make it back for Christmas and the timing was tight. After many hugs we waved off my sister and her family at the dock, dingied to the boat and weighed anchor. The northerly breeze sent us south to the amazing waters of the pristine Queensland holidays islets of the

Whitsundays and onward through the southern reaches of the Great Barrier Reef. This time the Queensland coast was stunning with perfect sailing conditions, an enormous improvement on our northbound journey 18 months prior.

But the trip through the northern parts of New South Wales were dominated by violent thunderstorms taking me back to the time in Singapore when that severe thunderstorm had threatened to end our journey. I was overcome by feelings of fear and a tightening in my stomach as I watched the bright white tongues of lightening lick the water close to the boat while we attempted to sail away from it. The storm circled around us for about an hour before dissipating. More storms and strong winds were to lash the coast as we continued our journey home, but we had good weather predictions and found safe harbour in the many coastal townships along New South Wales to avoid the worst of the weather.

The stormy weather dominated the final leg and we stopped to wait for calmer conditions a number of times. So the trip was slow and on 21 December 2015, almost three months after we had arrived in Cairns, we departed Nelson Bay for the short 90 mile overnight sail to Sydney - we were going to make it to Sydney for Christmas after all.

I was on watch for my shift as the eastern horizon sparkled with a line of light pink, it was the dawning of a new day and our day to arrive home to Sydney. I was overcome with a range of emotions but I think my most dominant feeling was one was relief. The next was a sense of joy at coming home - and the city did put on her best dress for us, shining in the glow of the new morning. The city was stretching its legs and arms to wake to a spectacular day and it was somewhat more spectacular for us as we rubbed our tired eyes and warmed our hands in the chilly summer morning air. It was just us and the first ferries of the day as we sailed down a flat and calm Sydney Harbour making our way towards the iconic Opera House and Harbour Bridge. The glass buildings were changing face from a silvery exterior to a golden one; as the sun rose higher and higher in the sky they cast fingers of reflection off their façades through the morning haze. The sail through the harbour took a while and we were able to soak it up and enjoy the feeling of being back in our own backyard, the place where it all began. We glided underneath the Sydney Harbour bridge and safe to say, we were both extremely elated.

We were finally completing a journey that had started 20 months before. We had covered 13,000 nautical miles. Plus we had done something that not many people do, we went east, against the trade winds – the hard way, to bring the boat back from South East Asia.

The next thing we had to plan was what the new year held for us, we had to think about what we would do for work and where would we live. No more planning of sailing routes or weather watching, we had returned and our new life awaited us. We'd dropped the anchor. We'd made it home.

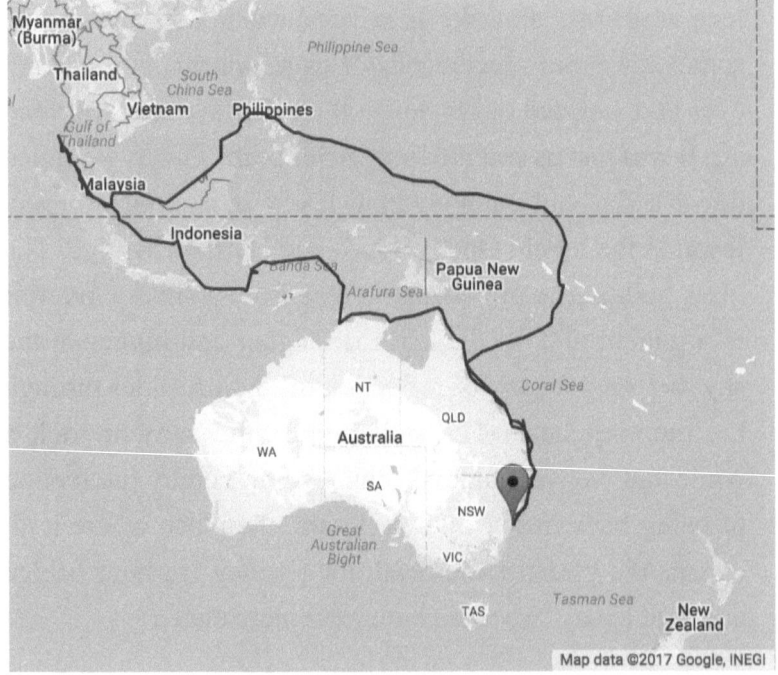

Map of our 13,000 nm journey

Post Script

Reflecting on the three years since we sailed *Elizabeth Jane II* back in through Sydney heads, so much has happened. Initially we spent six months on our boat moored in Sydney, living by night as cruisers and by day working in new jobs. It was a funny mix of lifestyles. We would dingy to shore in our smart clothes, change from thongs into work shoes and hop on the bus to the city each day, hoping that it wasn't pouring with rain or that we wouldn't get swamped by a wave from a passing ferry.

When we set out on the trip, it was never supposed to be forever, more a break from our normal lives. So while we returned to the fields of profession we had been working in before leaving, this time we were refreshed and invigorated really enjoying our jobs. I think it was about the feeling of contributing, of being busy, a stark contrast to some of the feelings that I had while on the boat – times where I had this overwhelming feeling of guilt for our privilege and opportunity to be on the holiday for such a long time. We had so much more than the people had in the places that we visited, but we hoped that our tourism would give a little. Returning to work kept us busy and started our reintegration back into the society which we had left. I had to relearn to wear shoes, brush my hair, and for the first time in two years, buy a phone and a wallet. Learning to live by a clock rather than tide times was another change to accept.

Shortly after arriving back we found out that I was pregnant. It was then, as I was afflicted with terrible morning sickness, that we decided to move back to land, so once again we became land lubbers. After a little while we found that we were not spending enough time on the boat and couldn't bear to watch her degrade on a mooring, so reluctantly decided to sell her.

We tied the knot a year later in the company of family and friends, reminiscing about Hugh's elaborate and romantic engagement proposal in remote Micronesia. Now having two energetic little boys we are looking back on some inspiring fellow cruisers that we met on our journey, including cruising families who thought that there was no better way to invest in their children than to take them travelling and spend time with them in new places. The idea of living life and exploring the world as a family has really resonated with us. We are now working and saving hard to go out cruising again, this time as a family before our boys get much older. For our next voyage we hope to embark on a slow sail west from the United States across the Pacific Ocean to Australia, and then who knows, maybe further. We have definitely caught the cruising bug!

So how did I change? It's not obvious, not something immediately perceivable. But I have a different attitude to life, about being more relaxed and accepting of change and things not going to plan. I think this has definitely been an important trait of becoming a parent, as children rarely follow any rule book. Also the opportunity to meet so many different people of different cultures and seeing their lifestyle and living conditions has really rammed home how lucky we are to live here. In a stable country politically, to have freedoms and have the abundant access to food, health care and education the way that we do. The experience has left us with a thirst to see more of the world by boat and despite the challenges of sailing, the experiences we will have in the places we visit will overcome all of that.

There was no secret to our success, we were lucky with the weather but also thoughtful with our times of departure and assessing conditions. The boat was a great boat and Hugh selected it well, it had a good ocean going reputation and while there were hundreds of tiny annoying things about it – like the spaghetti of electrical wiring that constantly required medical attention, it was an excellent cruising boat that had been well cared for. Some people have a morning health routine, we had a morning boat health routine – Hugh would check the oil in the engine, test run the engine, check the batteries, check the anchor hold, review the weather to make sure we weren't in for nasty changes and then settle down for breakfast. It made for early problem identification and a long to-do list for maintenance. We had lots of things fail, the fridge, the batteries, the wiring to connect the solar panels and then the wind generator to the batteries, the engine cooling impeller exploding and so many more, and without the knowledge and advice from fellow cruisers or our compendium of 'how-to-DIY-fixit' books we may not have been able to solve some of our problems. Things go wrong, it's inevitable. You just have to take it as it comes and enjoy the ride.

www.ingramcontent.com/pod-product-compliance
Lightning Source LLC
Chambersburg PA
CBHW030529010526
44110CB00048B/787